The Lemming CONSPIRACY

HOW TO REDIRECT YOUR LIFE FROM STRESS TO BALANCE

BOB D. MCDONALD, PH.D., *and* DON HUTCHESON

LONGSTREET PRESS, INC.
Atlanta, Georgia

Published by
LONGSTREET PRESS, INC.
A subsidiary of Cox Newspapers
A subsidiary of Cox Enterprises, Inc.
2140 Newmarket Parkway
Suite 122
Marietta, GA 30067

Printed in the United States of America

1st printing 1997

Library of Congress Catalog Card Number: 97-71930

ISBN: 1-56352-423-6

Jacket design and book graphics by Don and Tina Trousdell / The
    Triangle Company
Electronic film prep by OGI, Forest Park, GA
Book design by Jill Dible

This book is dedicated to —

Donald Super, Ph.D.

John Crystal

Johnson O'Connor

Murray Bowen, M.D., and

Daniel Levinson, Ph.D.,

thinkers far ahead of their times.

ACKNOWLEDGMENTS

Our Highlands Program staff, our network of Licensees, and our investors all took a personal and professional chance on an unproven and untried idea. All had the instinct and foresight to look into the future.

We would like to thank our Highlands Program staff, consultants, and professionals. We would not have been able to accomplish building our company without them: Shelly Danz, Laleah Henderson, Lanie Damon, Ann Dangar, Barbara Doty, Wieda Duncan, Micky Land, Natalie Gold, LeAnn Ransbotham, Meg Smith, Linda Merrion, Lisa Morris, Dori Stiles, Chris McGinnis, Cynthia Lynch, Andy McBride, Charlotte Hayes, Robin Hirsch, Paige Moody, and Tina Matera.

We would also like to thank our growing network of Highlands Program Licensees and their staffs. Their high standards of service delivery and constant attention to quality are what make our program great. Our current Licensees: Susan B. Andrews, Ph.D., Don Adams, Ph.D., Sara Arroyo, Ph.D., Don Azevedo, Ph.D., Sharon Balcome, Ph.D., Gregory Boardman, M.Ed., Ann Brody, M.S.W., Sookyung Chang, Ph.D., Denny Charlton, Ph.D., Steven J. Chen, Ph.D., James Ferguson, M.D., David Cox, Ph.D., Michael Darnell, D. Phil., Dan Dworkin, Ph.D., David Elkins, Ph.D., Ronald M. Sohr, Shelley Forman, M.A., M.B.A., Michael H. Foust, Ph.D., Adam K. Fuller, Ph.D., Dennis Kogut, Ph.D., Timothy Gunther, M.S., M.Div., Lynn W. Hamby, M.A., Sean F. Harrington, M.A., Hannah Jacobson, M.S.S., Sunaina R. Jain, Ph.D., James E. Jennings, Ph.D., Nancy D. Johnson, M.S., Stuart Kantor, Ph.D., Carol R. Kelly, Ph.D., Nevin Lantz, Ph.D., Edward Latham, Ph.D., Cheryl Leitschuh, Ed.D., Karen Logan, M.A., John Long, Ph.D., David MacRae, Ph.D., Ken Manges, Ph.D., Randy Marston, M.A., Leslie F. Martel, Ph.D., Leslie Martin, Joy McCarthy, Ph.D., Daniel Melbourne, Ph.D., Alfonse L. Mercatante, M.Ed., Linda K. Merrion, M.S., Ellen Moran, Ph.D., Ronald J. Murphy, Ph.D., Collin A. Myers. Ph.D., Timothy Orrell, Ph.D., Ted Papperman, Ph.D., Sharon H. Patterson, Ph.D., W. Randall Patton, M.A., N.C.C., Kim Payton, Ph.D., Hy Pomerance, Psy.D., Debra Robinson, Ph.D., Robert P. Rosen, M.S., Richard U. Rosenfield, Ph.D., William J. Rowell, Ph.D., T. Scott Sewitch, Ph.D., Arnold Holzman, Ph.D., Jeffrey Siegel, Ph.D., Carole E. Smith, M.A., M.S., Bill Southerland, Dick Blackwell, Ph.D., Jeffrey F. Spar, Ph.D.,

Steven M. Warner, Ph.D., Dori Stiles, Ph.D., Nancy Sutton, Ph.D., David Sweet, Ph.D., Thomas N. Tavantzis, Ed.D., Jerry Thompson, Ed.S., Gary Tyson, Ph.D., David Vickery, Ph.D., Emily Wang, Ph.D, Beverly Gay Weekes, Ph.D., D. Kent Welsh, Ph.D., Ronald Westrate, Ph.D., and Dave Wickstrom, Ph.D.

We also appreciate Jake Gibbs, Angelina Corbet and our growing network of marketing partners.

In addition, the following people had the insight to see the power of our idea as a business very early in its development: Stewart Alston, Pam and Ken Bonning, Robert and Suzi Curry, Jeannie and Richard DuBose, Daniel Dworkin, Michael and Vivianna Foust, Thomas Frisbie, Don Hutcheson, Sr., Frank Inman, David and Linda Ivey, Stuart Kantor, Eileen Keough, Micky Land, Linda Lee, James McAfee, Allen McDonald, Paul McDonald, Ronald and Ellen Murphy, Godfrey Newton, Jane Shivers, Virginia Soules, David Sweet, Robert and Cynthia Turoff, Marcia Weber, Ruth West, and Robert Ziegler, Jr.

Patti Hulvershorn believed in this idea and in our ability to make a business out of it from the very beginning.

Ketchum Communications has been instrumental in helping us increase awareness of and response to a new and complex idea and service. The intelligence, good will and immense knowledge of Jane Shivers, Robyn Freedman, Alexis Davis, Jenny Denee and Russ Williams have been invaluable.

David Ivey, Jeffrey Haidet, Stephen Camp, Deborah Stone, Jan Smith and Barbara Mills of Long, Aldridge & Norman have provided invaluable counsel and great personal support through the years of building our company.

Robert Arogeti of Habif, Arogeti, & Wynne has helped us take the hard financial looks at our company that have kept us on track.

We would like to thank Tamara Fiveashe-Watkins for her support and insight as our banker.

We would like to thank Elizabeth Lyon for her wonderful editorial work with our manuscript.
We want to thank Chuck Perry, John Yow, Jeannie Tarkenton, and

Marge McDonald of Longstreet Press. We appreciate their taking such time and painstaking effort with two untried authors.

A number of people have supported and nurtured our program over the years, for which we are ever grateful. This listing is necessarily incomplete. Harris Warsaw, Jerry Cushing, Susan Rinaldi, Tom Smith and Mary E. Haley of IBM, Ray Shaw, of the American City Business Journals, Ed Baker, David Rubinger, and Carl Wooten of the *Atlanta Business Chronicle*, Tim Bayless and Gary Kaczmarek of Bayless and Partners, Brenda Brown and Earl Gurr of Brown & Spiegel, Nancy Bryan, Carolyn Jerdan, Nancy Cole, Missy Sanchez, Thrower Starr, Jean Hague, Jacque Damgaard, Kathy Doherty, Libby Eason, Karen Tedeschi, Zoe Reichmann, Tracie Stein, Brian Bailey, Brad Kibler, Robert Holmes, William Cochran, Joe Dennis, Frank MacConochie, Kenneth Menendez, Cheryl Mure, Chris Miller, Alf Nucifora, Don and Tina Trousdell, Bob Morrison (the writer), Marcia White, Vicki Mowery, Elizabeth Chambers, Margaret Hutchison, Joy McCarthy, Ellen Wolchansky, Dianne Grove, Dana Brooks Brown, Tina Hertensen, Mendy McConnell, Marjorie Jordan, Henry Mullins, Bianca Quantrell, Chip Cipolla, Le Trombetta, Paul Sanger, Ed Augustine, Dana Brooks Brown, Lorelei Robbins, Betsy Richards, Todd Stansbury, Rob Taylor, Shawn Seale, Larkin Fowler, Rob Winborne, and Tom Traeger—all had the vision to see the power of our ideas to help people.

In addition, Bob would especially like to thank the following very important people who have supported his career change at this life Turning Point: his brothers, Allen and Paul, and their wives, Ann Carter and Becky; his children, Peter and Erin; and especially his wife, Susan. To Susan: "I could not imagine having taken this journey without your continuing support and love. Nor would I have wanted to."

Don would like to thank: Don Evans Hutcheson, Sr., Betty Stallworth Hutcheson, Mary Linda Lee, Evan Elisabeth Lee, Matthew Ryan Lee, Lindsay Allyn Lee, Pamela Elaine Bonning, Ralph Marconi Stallworth, Mary Kinard Stallworth, Jane Edwards Shivers, Will Davis Shivers, Clay Houston Shivers, Chandler K. McDougall, Joe Lo Curto, Dan and JoAnn Goodchild, Marcia and Charlie Weber, James Moore, Sue Symons, Zoe Reichmann, Brian Bailey, Michael and Vivianna Foust, Jacque Damgaard, Brenda Brown and Lynda Clark. "Thanks for always being there. You each give meaning to my life."

CONTENTS

INTRODUCTION

IN LEGEND, THE SMALL ARCTIC MAMMALS KNOWN as lemmings band together from time to time and, running in vast herds, throw themselves over cliffs to their deaths. As a metaphor, it seems to describe how too many of us live our lives, the authors included.

In August 1990, as two 42-year-old men, each successful, but in entirely different fields, we quit our jobs and spent the next two years researching and developing a program to help people figure out what to do with their lives—and how to escape the Lemming Conspiracy.

Coming at the problem from totally different perspectives (Bob's background is psychology, while Don's is business, advertising, and publishing), we personally underwent, experienced and participated in every test, service or program we could find that would bear on the question: What do you want to do with your life?

One fact became clear to us in all of this research. The question of what to do with your life is much larger and more complicated than most people realize. In our imaginations, perhaps, we think that most people just make a decision about career sometime in their early twenties, and then proceed to do that for the rest of their working lives.

Nothing could be further from the truth. Deciding upon a career has become an agonizing question for high school and college students. Many we talked to (and we talked to hundreds in our research) had no idea what they wanted to do, dreaded the thought of leaving college and entering the adult world, and thought of graduate and professional schools as a way to delay the ultimate question a little longer. Almost all were anxious about how to see themselves clearly in the adult world.

It's well known that college students have a tough time trying to figure out a plan for their lives; statistics on dropout, transfer, and underemployment among college students and graduates speak for themselves. What may be surprising is that we never fully settle the question for all time. We go through six major Turning Points in our adult working lives, from our early twenties to our sixties. And they don't stop with retirement. *We continue to experience Turning Points in our seventies and eighties.* About every seven to ten years, we make important decisions about our careers for our entire adult lives. At each of these Turning Points, we recreate ourselves. But most of the time, we never look at our most creative and powerful options. We see ourselves far too narrowly. We become lemmings.

We, the authors, speak from experience. We were both the original lemmings. Our college choices, career choices, career moves, and life decisions were perfect expressions of the Lemming Conspiracy.

In our research, we discovered that while many talented people had developed excellent career-counseling programs, none of them addressed the whole question of planning for a life. We thought that if we could develop a program that systematically addressed *all* of the important career and life decision factors, *and* if we could help people pull together and integrate all of these complex issues, then we could provide a highly useful service to people at any major Turning Point, from high school, through mid-life, to retirement, and beyond.

We did develop this program, and we launched it in 1992. Response from our clients has been overwhelmingly positive. We began licensing this program in 1994 to psychologists and counselors all over the country, and we now have offices in most major cities nationwide. We have also recently developed and launched a corporate version of this same program for executives and managers to help them clarify their visions of their own careers and align these visions with their companies' missions.

We wrote this book to alert people to the vital importance and life-changing power of creating and using a Personal Vision to direct their lives, and we have designed a step-by-step process for developing this Personal Vision. By this means we hope to achieve our ultimate goal: to help people escape the stifling effects of the Lemming Conspiracy and live the lives that, in their innermost hearts, they want to lead.

"Fearful of what lay ahead, but even more afraid of complete isolation, [the Lemming] threw himself into the crowd. It was defeat, and [he] knew it, but it was mixed with great relief. All decisions were gone. So was concern for the future, so was the fear of conflicting with his own kind."

Alan Arkin, THE LEMMING CONDITION

CHAPTER 1

The Lemming CONSPIRACY

WHAT IF WE TOLD YOU ABOUT A CONSPIRACY, widespread and insidious, that controlled what you do every day and even how you feel about what you do? What if this conspiracy controlled your perceptions of yourself and of options in your career?

Such a conspiracy routinely invades almost every aspect of all our lives. Born of benign intentions, but almost totally hidden from our awareness, it operates outside of our conscious will and keeps us from knowing who we are and what we could really do in the world.

Why do all of us settle for lives that are stressful, unfulfilling and often empty of meaning? Why do we spend our energy and time acquiring possessions that bring us so little happiness in the end? Why do we ignore people who are important to us, and ignore ourselves in the bargain? We behave in these "irrational" ways because the Lemming Conspiracy keeps us from experiencing ourselves as we really are.

We grow up learning to see a limited range of options as if it constituted *all* our options. Our schools, colleges, corporations, organizations, friends and families actively work to encourage this limited view throughout our lives. Why? Not because they are evil, certainly, but because they are systems. Systems create and carry out the Lemming Conspiracy.

HOW SYSTEMS CONTROL OUR PERCEPTIONS OF OURSELVES

The fundamental fact about all systems is this: Any system of which you are a member has its own goals and interests, and those goals and interests are not the same as your goals and interests.

> NOTE: In this book, we will often talk about systems having goals, systems wanting things, or systems in other ways behaving as though they were alive. A system is a way of describing how people work together in stable groups like families or corporations. Obviously, it is an abstraction, and has no will or wants of its own. But systems act as though they do have a life of their own. Many systems routinely produce results *exactly the opposite* of those that each and every person in the system wants to produce.

AN OFFICE SYSTEM

At the very simplest level, everyone in a typical corporate office goes to work at about the same time every day, works steadily during the morning, takes off for lunch at about the same time, works steadily during the afternoon, and finishes the day's work at about the same time. Everyone in the office knows that they have choices about what they do all day long. But they act as though their choices were limited. In order to be members of this particular system—this office—they have to go by the rules. Otherwise the system will not function.

But there are other rules that are less overt and which therefore work more powerfully. Some examples of the kind of unstated rules you might find in an office:

- You should strive to make more money and gain a higher position in the organization.
- You must give up significant aspects of your personal life in order to be successful.
- If you don't get promoted, you are a failure.
- Work is not something you should think about enjoying; that's why they call it work.
- You should do whatever it takes to succeed, including 12-hour days and 75-hour weeks.
- Work hard, play by the rules, and you will be successful and happy.
- Happiness has something to do with how much you can buy.

These rules, powerful but covert, are different for every system, but they make systems work.

If everyone *didn't* act as though moving up the corporate hierarchy and being able to buy a better car were important, then the young people in the company wouldn't be scrambling all over each other trying to compete for the top spots. They wouldn't be willing to put up with drudgery and meaningless labor in order to please someone they might not respect. Middle-aged managers who want something more in their lives might begin to look outside the corporation. The collapse of the corporation would follow, with civilization not far behind—at least, this seems to be the driving fear that motivates systems to remain ever the same.

The *system* acts as though its rules are reality. It acts as though you as a member of a system fully buy into and share all of its rules. Systems are conservative; they don't change their rules easily or often. Surface appearances of change rarely, if ever, change the fundamental rules of any system. As a member of a system, you are under a great deal of pressure to believe, buy into, and live out its rules. And most people do.

Subtly and silently, or overtly and crassly, systems encourage employees to forget about their interests and passions when they go to work, and to think of their life goals in terms of money and promotions. They are not encouraged to explore and develop natural gifts and talents. They are even discouraged from looking very closely at their deepest values. At work people are often discouraged from self-exploration in general.

Systems act as though each person is a collection of skills and functions. They operate most effectively when you see yourself in this way, too. You remain distant from yourself, defining yourself firmly in one way, when the reality of yourself may be different entirely. This situation creates and perpetuates the Lemming Conspiracy.

HOW THE LEMMING CONSPIRACY BEGINS—THE FAMILY OF ORIGIN

The Lemming Conspiracy begins in the family of origin as the families in which we grow up give us a primary sense of who we are. This happens outside of anyone's awareness, but it is a fundamental fact of development. Our perceptions of ourselves as smart, stupid, good-looking, capable, incapable, affiliative, distant and all of the hundreds of other ways we describe and think about ourselves start forming by about age four. They become solidified by the time we are 18 and ready to move out of our family homes into the wider world.

Children absorb a sense of who they are and what they "ought" to be doing in the world from their parents. This influence is often rejected by the rebellious teen: "I don't know who I am, but I know who I am *not*. I am not like my father." What is hidden from the teenager who might mutter such a thought is that *his* father, when he was 18, probably had exactly the same thought about his own father.

Sometime around age 30 to 35, people often realize, with some horror, "I have become my parent." This recognition frequently occurs after they have children of their own. These people have, of course, been like their parents all along without realizing it. Their first conscious memories are of when they were five or six years old and their parents were 30 to 35. When recognition strikes, they are just recalling their first memories of their parents.

This process of acquiring a fully formed image of ourselves, a picture which includes both parents, is almost completely unconscious, but is one of the most powerful forces in our lives. It is called *identification*. It is the fully formed picture of who we are that we learn in our families of origin, and then take into adulthood. Without it, people could not grow up. They could not leave their families. They could not form ties and relationships in the adult world. They would not know the "rules" of adult life.

This image of ourselves makes it possible to enter the adult world, and creating it is the main function of the family system. But this image also limits. We not only learn who we *are* in families, but we also learn who we are *not*. We learn, clearly, what role we are to play in the adult world, and we learn how to play it. Already, in the family system, we start to see divergence between how our *system* sees us and the potential we see in ourselves. Later, we will talk about the difference between our System Selves, the self that the system sees, and our True Selves, the person we are able to be.

The family of origin is a system. It is a closed circle of relationships that has its own history, rules, roles and customs. All of these remain stable over time. If you study a family for many years, you will see that certain roles and types keep reappearing generation after generation. When we leave home we take our "model" of the family system out into the world and recreate it when we start our own families.

Our family model is also the model for any other system that we become involved in, join, or create throughout our lives. We join systems that "fit." We choose our friends, churches, synagogues, clubs, organizations, schools, companies and corporations, and they choose us, because they fit, and we fit. There is a role we can play in the system that we learned in our families of origin. This role may be exactly right for us. It may tap into every one of our natural talents and satisfy our deepest goals in life. It may perfectly express our fundamental values and involve aspects of life that we find intrinsically fascinating.

Or not. We learn roles in our families of origin that have more or less to do with our personal makeup. As we enter the adult world, we usually discover much more about ourselves than our families typically see. But our families, and other systems in which we become involved, persistently see us in stable interpersonal roles. These perceptions don't change easily.

All systems strongly encourage you to see yourself as *they* see you. If you seamlessly fulfill your role, then the system operates more smoothly, if not more creatively. The problem is, *you* get lost, and it is difficult to get another view of yourself as long as you are involved in the normal systems of your life.

What follows is a true story about a person who did everything right. She went to the right schools, made wonderful grades, got a great job, and was successful at every turn. While she lived out a life her systems encouraged her to live, she steadily lost a true sense of herself and what she wanted from her life. Although she didn't realize it, she was a victim of the Lemming Conspiracy.

> NOTE: We will tell much of the story of this book through the stories of people's lives. In all cases, the stories are based on real people and the actual events of their lives; however, we have changed their names and any possible identifying information about them in order to protect their privacy.

Sara's Story

Sara grew up in a small town in Minnesota. An excellent student in high school, she had many extracurricular interests, including theater, which she loved. School came so easily that she seldom worked hard. Theater consumed a far more important share of her time and creative talent than academics.

Sara's father, a successful computer systems analyst, had gone to graduate school right after college, intending to get a Ph.D. in history. At the time he dreamed of teaching. When he earned his master's degree he did teach for a while.

Teaching made him happy, but he realized that he could never earn a high salary in this field. He had been married two years and had a little daughter for whom he was responsible. *His* father's image, that of a man providing well for his family, forcefully urged him to change.

Sara's father switched to computers, and soon was doing well financially. When he took a job, he generally liked it at first, but it quickly became routine. There was nothing intrinsically interesting to him about computers or computer systems. When his unhappiness reached the breaking point, he would find a new job. To him this did not seem unusual. He assumed most people didn't really like their jobs.

Sara's mother was also a successful computer systems consultant. She didn't find her work rewarding either—just lucrative. She had stayed in the same job with the same firm for many years and was considered quite good at her role. She didn't find her work particularly interesting, creative or fun. It was work, and she did it, and was happy to have a job.

Sara's mother had a love, too. She created handmade clothes for children. She had quite a following among her friends and had opened a shop to sell her creations. She loved all aspects of this endeavor—from the fabrics and their colors, to the design and creation of the clothes, to helping people find exactly the right garment for a family or a child. But she didn't call it work. It was a hobby. In her lexicon, work was what you had to do. Whether you enjoyed it or not was completely beside the point.

And so Sara went off to college. She went to a small, select, liberal arts college in the South and did well—3.8 average. "I figured out very quickly what I needed to do to get an 'A'. I just took the right courses and paid attention in class and always did just enough to slide under the wire. I took history courses and English courses, but what I really enjoyed was drama. I got involved in a theater group the first semester I was on campus. It held the whole focus of my attention throughout four years of college. I loved the life of the theater; I loved the people in theater; I loved everything about it. It easily absorbed 90 percent of my attention and energy."

Sara never thought about what she would do after college. Even well into her senior year, she did not have a real idea about what she would do when she graduated. An advisor, looking at her transcript, asked her if she had ever thought about law school. She had not. She had never, as far as she could remember, even known a lawyer. But this seemed like a plan.

Sara applied to six law schools and was accepted by four, among them Yale. She decided to go there. Why? "It's *Yale*. You can't turn down Yale." She walked onto the Yale campus the next fall never having interviewed a lawyer, or worked in a lawyer's office, or even wondered too much about what a lawyer did. She just thought it would be a way to make money.

"I knew as soon as I started that I hated law. But, once again, I could make A's fairly easily. I did just as much as was necessary, nothing more. I joined a theater group right away, and the great majority of my time and energy went there. The saddest day of my life was the day I graduated from law school. It meant that I would have to stop doing what I really like to do in life and start working to pay back my law-school debts."

Sara's story was published on the front page of a major metropolitan newspaper, because she had secured a job in a distinguished law firm well before graduation, and because she had produced and directed a video about law students, which was broadcast on PBS. In the video, students talk about law and law school, and their feelings of anger and frustration at being trapped in a profession they don't like, have no real interest in, but which will pay them well anyway.

We talked to Sara about a year after she started working for the firm. As a young associate she had had so little time that she couldn't be involved in the theater. She succeeded in the firm, but was already thinking that if she moved to New York City, she could earn more money, save it faster, and eventually be able to do what she wanted.

Obviously, Sara had absorbed a great deal from her mother and father. On the positive side, she was talented, worked hard, and did well at whatever she set out to do. On the negative side, she had absorbed both parents' pattern of being in work they didn't like and had no interest in. She would use her father's pattern of changing jobs in order to deal with her present unhappiness and dissatisfaction. And it would probably work no better for her than it did for her father. Her parents had given her the answers they habitually used, and she had taken them over without realizing it.

Sara left her family of origin and established herself independently. By almost any yardstick she had succeeded, and her family had successfully performed its main role and function.

But no system ever challenged Sara's basic assumptions or her decisions. Nor could it. This fundamental limitation of systems is the defining fact of the Lemming Conspiracy.

From the point of view of Sara's high school, everything was fine. One of their brightest seniors went to an excellent liberal arts college. For them to challenge whether it was the right school, with enough options to explore what she really loved, would be madness. She had done well academically; she had been accepted to a strongly academic institution: Perfect.

At college, once again, everything appeared to be fine and on course. How could anyone think there was a problem? Sara *herself* didn't think there was a problem. It was only when the end of her senior year loomed that any troubling thoughts came to her. What would she do *now?* Her advisor saw a bright, verbally oriented student with excellent grades, and one clear answer popped into his head—law school. She could get in, and it would make the college look good. The fact that she ended up going to Yale made it so much the better.

For the school to challenge this situation would be foolish in the extreme. As a small, very selective, expensive liberal arts institution, the school's survival depended on its graduates getting into graduate and professional schools. Getting graduates into *Yale* validated the fundamental premise of the school: "We are doing a good job because our graduates go on to high-quality graduate and professional programs."

Yale certainly never challenged Sara's decision. It was happy to have such a bright student. It was even happier, as an institution, when one of its brighter and more talented students landed a good job four months before graduation. *That* makes a school look good.

The firm in which she landed saw its future in being able to attract smart, talented young lawyers who would work like demons for five to seven years until they are hooked into the financial rewards. Landing a Yale student near the top of her class, a *female*, was exactly what the firm wanted to do. And did.

All of these systems—high school, college, professional school, law firm—had their own goals and their own interests. Sara was precisely fulfilling these interests and goals for each of these systems. But these systems' interests were clearly not the same as Sara's interests—not even close. And Sara had never looked at what her own interests and goals might be. Nor was she encouraged to. Instead, she was encouraged to think of herself as bright, successful and on the way to the top. When we, the authors, met her, she was unhappy and feeling trapped by debt. The only escape she could imagine was the exact answer her father had used to keep himself unhappy and trapped most of his career.

HOW WE GET OUT OF BALANCE AND HOW THAT LEADS TO STRESS

Sara's story, that of a young person who goes from success to success to success and yet ends up feeling trapped and unhappy, shows in clear relief how many people live out their lives in systems. While energetically jumping through hoop after hoop, they never stop to examine who they really are and what they really want from their lives.

With patterns and roles absorbed from our families of origin, we leap into the world in our early twenties. We find systems to join that fit our sense of ourselves and our sense of what roles we could play in life. This works well for systems, and it appears to work pretty well for us—for a while.

Throughout our adult lives, we experience regular cycles of stability and change. We launch ourselves into the beginning of our careers, just like Sara did. At first everything may seem fine. We may feel that we are a good match for a system at the beginning. The system's values appear to match our own. Our lives seem interesting and exciting.

With each passing year, we grow and change. We become different on the inside. We have new ideas, meet new people, have new goals, and new wants. But the systems in which we remain do not change their views of us. To our systems (and this includes our family systems) we are the same. Our systems assume we have remained on the same path, that we have the same buy-in to the system's values and rules.

SYSTEM SELF, TRUE SELF AND LIFE BALANCE

This increasing disparity between ourselves as our systems see us and ourselves on the inside—the difference between the

System Self and the *True Self*—leads to our becoming increasingly out of balance. In general, we have a choice. We can either struggle with our systems about how they define us and how we define ourselves, or we can increasingly see ourselves as our systems see us. Very few people end up struggling with systems—at least, not for very long.

SYSTEM SELF

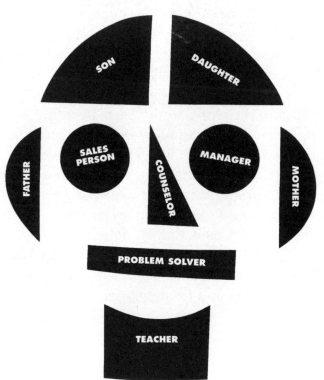

THE ROLE OR FUNCTION THE SYSTEM SEES

We *become* who our systems think we are. This invariably means that we are not attending to or putting enough energy into one or more critically important elements of our lives. Systems have only a limited view of us. We are whole people, but systems see only roles and functions. How many middle-aged men have awakened in the middle of the night with the nightmarish realization that the way they are spending their lives and energy feels utterly meaningless? How many middle-aged women have suddenly seen their lives as without meaning when their children leave home? Or how many hard-driving professional women wake up in their early thirties and realize that they forgot to have children?

TRUE SELF

THE WHOLE SELF THAT IS POSSIBLE

The Lemming Conspiracy captured them all and anesthetized them. These middle-aged people suddenly wake to discover what has really been going on for a number of years: their System Selves, defined by the role or function that the system demands, and their True Selves, the whole person that is possible, have grown irreparably apart.

The result of this disparity? Stress. Also anxiety, anger and often depression. When the stress or anxiety reaches some critical point, it often starts to seep into awareness. It is at these times of greater awareness—times we call Turning Points—that we seek new answers and change.

We *could* find creative answers and new directions at Turning Points, but too often we do not, because the Lemming Conspiracy still holds us captive.

TURNING POINTS AND LIFE CHANGES

As we reach the critical point of stress and anxiety, we arrive at a *Turning Point*. At Turning Points we feel ready for change. We actively seek new answers. One of the best-known Turning Points arrives at mid-life, but there are actually eight of them. With remarkable regularity, they come every seven to ten years throughout our adult lives. These all-important crises of adult life can lead to positive creativity and change, but all too often do not.

At Turning Points, we are often aware of the increasing disparity between who we are and what our systems see. And we often try to change something. But what? The answers come from the family of origin. We will invariably make the same kind of decision, and for about the same reason, as one or the other of our parents made at the same age. We will talk more about Turning Points and how we typically make these decisions in Chapter Three.

In Sara's story above, we can see the pattern of decision-making at Turning Points—both for Sara and her parents. At the critical Turning Point at the start of adulthood, she decided to go into a field that was financially secure but offered little personal reward, just as her father did. Her sense of what work is and should be was formed by what she observed in her mother and father. She was well on her way to repeating her father's strategy of dealing with stress.

We could predict that it would be no more successful with her than it was with her father.

We can see these same forces at work with a young man named Mitchell at a later Turning Point. He became increasingly aware of the disparity between his System Self and his True Self and was moved to change. The first answers he thought of came straight from his family of origin, just as they would for anyone. They could easily have led him to repeat Sara's mistake, but Mitchell took a new path, and his story ends differently from Sara's.

Mitchell's Story

Mitchell started working for a large technology firm straight out of college. He energetically pursued his career and achieved success early. He worked predominantly in sales. He came to the attention of his bosses and they wanted him on the fast track. "By age 30, I liked what I was doing. I liked my co-workers and clients. The company had been good to me, but I just felt this restlessness and uneasiness I couldn't put my finger on."

The firm could not help Mitchell with this problem. All of its answers are in the interest of the firm, not of Mitchell. Obviously, as long as Mitchell is productive, his firm will encourage him to "stay the course." It is in its interests for Mitchell to think that a good job, good pay, and good co-workers are enough. That is exactly what Mitchell thought. Or, more correctly, thought he should think.

Once this subtle misconception takes root, that a company's interests and a person's interests are the same thing, stress and imbalance loom on the horizon. Mitchell made this mistake when he tried to quiet his wish for change by admonishing himself to just grow up, settle down, and endure. Mitchell's firm could not help him figure out who he was and what he wanted. Mitchell was only aware of feeling that he had to do something different, and the fact that he was obviously successful just made his wish for change more stressful. Mitchell's True Self had diverged from his System Self, but he had no mechanism to find and identify his True Self. He had no way to use a vision of his True Self to stand up to his systems.

Mitchell's family couldn't help. The message from his parents could not have been more clear: "Are you crazy? Stay with your job. It's secure." He strongly felt the responsibility of his young child. He couldn't do anything that would jeopardize her. And yet he needed to do *something*.

Here, Mitchell's story departs from Sara's. Mitchell actively sought different answers by going through a structured process that systematically focused on all of the important factors of his life and career. It was crucial that the process did not involve his firm, his family or his circle of friends and colleagues. It was independent of all his systems and had no vested interest in the outcome of his search. As a result, it could help him come up with his own answers—what we call a Personal Vision—a fully articulated picture of his True Self. With a Personal Vision, Mitchell could escape the Lemming Conspiracy and start leading his own life.

What is a Personal Vision? What must it include to be effective in illuminating your True Self and defeating the Lemming Conspiracy? Eight critical factors must contribute. Leave one out, and you risk remaining entrapped.

Mitchell discovered what fit about his job and what did not fit, and why. He was able to use this insight to focus and position himself. He knew what he wanted to move away from; more important, he knew what tasks and roles he should go *toward*. He also knew why his systems' answers, although compelling, were not right for him. He was able to create a plan and make a significant move in his career to a position and role that he felt expressed him exactly. He says of his change: "My clients are happy, and I get to play from my strengths and my love. It is truly a wonderful fit."

In this book, we take you through the structured process Mitchell used to change his life and career. We created this process, and thousands of clients have used it successfully. It leads you to self-discovery. You must find your true natural talents and pull your hopes and dreams to daylight. You must identify your most potent skills and even journey back to your original family system. Finally, you will be able to use this process to create your own Personal Vision—your vision of your True Self.

Your Personal Vision must have a definite structure and form to be effective. Chapters Three through Seven take you through each of the eight critical factors, explaining what each is and what significance it has for your life. You will go through them in a definite order—from objective to subjective, external to internal.

The Thought Experiments at the end of each chapter help you translate the ideas of the chapters into a more practical reality. You can use these experiments as springboards for thought, or you can actually do the experiments. They are, at the very least, fascinating. They also hold the possibility of helping you transform your life.

Merely identifying and articulating the eight factors is not enough. A Personal Vision involves *creative integration*—a creative insight, if you will. Chapter Eight details the creative process we developed for our workshops and seminars. We call it *left-right-left*.

In the end a Personal Vision must relate to the real world if it is to help you live a balanced life. In Chapter Nine, we describe the process we use to accomplish this integration—Surveying. Surveying has incredible power to kick your Personal Vision into motion, to translate it to the reality of the marketplace.

Through all of these chapters, we tell the stories of four actual people at different Turning Points, all of whom go through the process of the book by completing the Thought Experiments. After each Thought Experiment, we revisit them to find out what they learned and how they use what they found out.

The final chapter talks about Personal Vision at different Turning Points; how it can help propel you into a new job; or how it can make your present job work better for you. We end with a discussion of the power of Personal Vision to transform corporations—to expand and open systems to make them more flexible, adaptable, and human.

NEXT CHAPTER: In the next chapter, we discuss the goal of the whole process, gaining a Personal Vision. A Personal Vision helps move you *out* of the cycle of stress, anger, and depression we call the Stress Cycle, and *toward* the more vital cycle of inner-directedness and balance we call the Balance Cycle.

CHAPTER 2

The Stress Cycle, the Balance Cycle and PERSONAL VISION

THE LEMMING CONSPIRACY LEADS INEVITABLY TO lives out of balance. Answers to the question of work and career learned in the family of origin help us move out into the adult world. But over time, they cease to be adequate. Our systems prevent us from recognizing and changing this situation. We develop an increasing disparity between our System Selves and our True Selves. Insofar as we ignore some important aspect of ourselves, let some important talent lie fallow, neglect a critical value, or do things for which we feel no intrinsic passion, we live in the Stress Cycle.

Most of the people you know live in the Stress Cycle, as you probably do yourself. The Lemming Conspiracy produces the Stress Cycle for nearly everyone sooner or later. Over time the Stress Cycle comes to rule people's lives.

This chapter shows how the Stress Cycle eventually captures each of us and how it comes to have such an overwhelming impact. But this chapter also tells you about the alternative, the Balance Cycle, and what it means to achieve it. We will describe the difficult task of moving from the Stress Cycle to the Balance Cycle and how a Personal Vision makes that journey possible. We will explain what a Personal Vision is and how you can create one for yourself. You'll learn how to beat the Lemming Conspiracy.

THE STRESS CYCLE

SOONER OR LATER, PEOPLE COME TO FEEL THAT THEIR LIVES MAINLY INVOLVE JUMPING THROUGH HOOPS.

When we are caught in the Stress Cycle, we feel like we are jumping through hoops. We work harder and gain little. Our day-to-day lives have little real meaning for us, even if we are engaged in work we *used* to enjoy. We have the uneasy feeling that something is missing, but it's difficult to identify what that might be. We have the definite sense that there is no time to think about any of this anyway. We barely have time to do what is absolutely necessary.

The hallmark of the Stress Cycle is its relentlessness. You never stop. A person in the Stress Cycle only has time to do the next task, or concentrate on the next project. There is no time for such "unproductive" work as thinking about your life or figuring out how you really want to spend your time.

If we operate in the Stress Cycle, we pass it on to our children. They see it as a normal and natural way for adults to exist in the world. We can tell them a thousand times that they can choose to live their lives any way they want to, and they don't have to choose the same answers we did. But we see a great many high school students already caught in the Stress Cycle. We see many who are seemingly trying with every ounce of strength to *avoid* falling prey to their parents' pattern. The hard fact is, that if *we* are in the Stress Cycle, sooner or later, *they* will be in the Stress Cycle, too.

How does the Stress Cycle start? Obviously no one would willingly and knowingly choose to live like this. No one would want their children to live like this. So why does virtually everyone do it?

The Stress Cycle emerges directly from systems and the Lemming Conspiracy. As we move into systems from our families of origin, there is an incredibly strong pull to *take the next step*. Declare a major. Graduate from college. Get a job, any job. Succeed. Earn more money. Buy more things. Move up in the organization. Complete the next project. Gain the boss's attention and approval. Become a boss. Retire. Die.

We are not talking about intelligence or character. We are talking about the universal pull of systems to engage us in the Stress Cycle. We are talking about how difficult it is to separate ourselves from this pull. Even people who routinely help others look at *their* long-term goals never think about whether their own lives are expressing a long-range vision.

So, what are the elements of the Stress Cycle? We have identified the following four:

> **1. Short-term focus.** Getting the next task done. "I'll just get this promotion, and *then I'll be able to live my life.*" Probably not. This focus on the task at hand means that

you are never able to focus on a larger context. What about your *life?* Most people spend far more time and energy focused on how they will spend their annual vacation than they do on how they will spend the next 20 or 40 years of their lives. *Systems want you to focus on the short-term goal. It is in their interest for you to do so.*

2. Status-driven goals. A new car would feel great. A new house. Maybe a second house. A promotion will mean that I'm getting somewhere in life. I want to dress like my bosses, and drive their cars. I want to have the kinds of lifestyles that I see in magazines and on television. I want more responsibility, so I can have more say in what happens. I want to be in charge, so I can have a life. *Systems want you to feel all of this. They want you to work very hard to achieve something that is basically empty of meaning, so that when you achieve it, you will focus on the next goal.*

3. Outer-directed priorities. Someone else tells you what is important. New car? Promotion? More money? Getting a college degree, earning a lot of money, gaining a position of responsibility and power—these are all worthy goals, *if* they are a direct expression of your Personal Vision. But, if they are not connected to anything larger in your life, they are empty, and you are being pulled along from hoop to hoop.

4. Reactive decision-making. Focusing only on short-term goals. Responding to everyday events as though to crises. When people concentrate only on short-term results, they become vulnerable to throwing all of their energy and creativity into problems that, in a longer view, may not be that important. Researchers in human behavior found long ago that getting people to concentrate on short-term reward resulted in increased short-term behavior. This narrowing of focus, however, inflates the importance of what may be trivial events. This inevitably leads to stress. How many people have led successful professional lives and accomplished each of their many goals only to discover, too late, that they never had a relationship with their children? Or their spouses? Or themselves, for that matter?

People in the Stress Cycle get caught up with achieving the next goal and accomplishing the next task. They feel too busy to examine their lives and figure out what might be personally meaningful. But people do not generally start out in the Stress Cycle. It develops over time.

HOW THE STRESS CYCLE TAKES OVER OUR LIVES

There are many high school students completely caught in the Stress Cycle. In academically competitive high schools, they are probably the majority. The Stress Cycle grips students even more firmly in college. As young men and women move out into the work world, marry, buy houses, cars, baby carriages and vacations, the Stress Cycle becomes as natural as breathing. Answers that worked reasonably well in the family of origin, and even for a while in adulthood, cease to function effectively. Consequently, stress develops.

When we live with chronic stress, we do not come up with creative answers. Our focus becomes short-term—we just want to get *this* job done, and then we can rest. We tend to focus on the goal in front of us. We do not feel we can take the time to think about what we are doing; we just need to do it. We tend to follow any direction presented to us. Unconsciously, we fall back on patterns learned in the family of origin. It is here that we start to become more and more like one of our parents, because we are making decisions exactly the way that parent made them at that age.

Below are the stories of two accomplished, successful professionals, Carol and Jane, both of whom had "succeeded" in the world through intelligence, planning, drive and character. You will also see that both were trapped in the Stress Cycle. Answers from their families of origin could not help them overcome the Lemming Conspiracy. Later, you will see how they figured out Personal Visions and started living more balanced lives.

Carol's story, below, shows how answers that started off working well eventually led to the Stress Cycle.

Carol's Story

When Carol was 38, she went through a structured process to gain a Personal Vision for her career. At the time, she was near burnout. She didn't think she would last two more years at her company. She didn't understand her stress and anxiety. She was still young; her job, if anything, was better than ever. But it just didn't feel like enough any more.

Carol's father had been a successful sales executive with a large company and had traveled throughout her childhood. A few years after she moved out of her family home, her parents divorced.

Like her father, Carol had always felt that her first responsibility was to be successful, but she had never challenged or even clearly articulated that perception.

Carol had never married or had a serious relationship longer than six months. She traveled three and four days a week. Almost anyone outside of Carol's family or network of busy professional friends strung out across the country could have told her that she would feel much better if she would create a life for herself outside of work. But her family and friends never challenged her assumptions, and her lifestyle prevented her from coming up with alternative answers.

Her bosses certainly didn't challenge her assumptions:

from their point of view, Carol was perfect. She was a high performer on the fast track, and probably had executive potential. The company had no way of knowing that Carol was considering quitting and that she was operating with markedly reduced efficiency and commitment as time went on. The company would never know until it became a crisis.

Carol had succeeded in forming an independent life for herself. She had succeeded in a competitive business, and could go all the way to the top. But she was caught in the Stress Cycle. Taking on the next project, accomplishing the next goal, pushing ahead with her career plan, she had left *herself* out of the formula. Now she was experiencing the stress, anxiety and sense of crisis that normally develop.

It would be impossible for the company to help her with this. The company's interests are different from Carol's; it cannot help her figure out who she is and what is important to her. Carol's response was absolutely typical: she redoubled her efforts, doing more of what she had always done. She used the same answers that had worked before.

These answers to her dilemma came from her family of origin; they could not help her. Carol's life mirrored her father's in many important ways. She had given over all her energy and focus to work, like her father, treating herself and her personal relationships as secondary to work. Also like him, she had not been able to develop a rewarding, fulfilling marriage or family.

Systems basically offer two answers at crisis points: do more of the same, or quit. As we have seen, Carol tried to do the first, and was considering the second as a real possibility. The next story is about Jane. It gives another view of systems' answers at Turning Points.

Business, social and family systems all nurture the forces leading to the Stress Cycle. Jane's story illustrates how the Stress Cycle can develop completely outside of business—but not outside of systems.

Jane's Story

Jane had raised two children; both went to college. She had always seen her role as supporting her husband's law career, a role she performed very well. He had started a successful firm, and her talents in connecting with people had been crucial to that success. She believed it was her responsibility to be available for her children and her husband.

Jane went through a structured career process at age 50. Her youngest son had come home from college the previous year. He had a job waiting tables. He spent most of his days watching MTV and soap operas and most of his nights with his friends. Her husband was seldom home, sometimes working seven days a week. She had no interests, plans or ideas about what to do with herself. She frequently had lunch with other lawyers' wives; their conversation felt pointless and mostly bored her. She started having migraine headaches that were stunningly debilitating.

Jane's mother had raised a large family in a small Southern town. Her father had been a minor public official. At about age 50, her mother developed a hip problem that prevented her from getting around. When her father died a few years later, it fell to Jane to take care of her mother full time, which she did until her mother died.

Jane was repeating her mother's life. A physical disability would take all choice away from her. Although her answers from her family of origin had worked well for years, they no longer helped her. Her husband couldn't help her; the Stress Cycle had ensnared him many years ago. Even her son was so caught in the family's stress that he could not form an independent life. It is interesting, and inevitable, that she would unconsciously choose her mother's solution to the problem—becoming incapacitated by illness—at about the same age her mother did.

Anyone can be a victim of the Stress Cycle, and in truth, almost everyone is at some point in their lives. But what is the alternative? We all live in systems. We all have to live in a stressful world. All of us get answers from our families of origin and then take them out into the world to start our lives. Those answers will eventually lead us to a crisis and a Turning Point.

These "crises" of our adult lives don't have to be negative. At these times we can become more open to change. We can look for new answers. Instead of adopting systems' answers or families' answers, we can use this openness to find *our own* answers. Over time, we can move from the Stress Cycle to the Balance Cycle.

THE BALANCE CYCLE

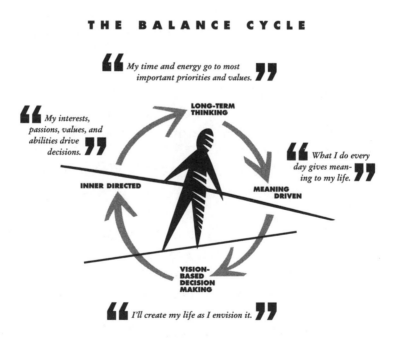

PEOPLE IN THE BALANCE CYCLE HAVE CREATED A POSITIVE
PERSONAL VISION FOR THE FUTURE.

Just as in the Stress Cycle, the elements of the Balance Cycle relate strongly to each other. One element leads to the next, and then to the next. It perpetuates itself, just like the Stress Cycle. And, we can pass along the Balance Cycle to our children, just like we can pass along the Stress Cycle.

So how does it work? What are the elements?

1. Long-term focus. Ultimately, anything you do should connect clearly to a fundamental value or goal. In the Balance Cycle, intermediate and short-term goals are steps toward a larger goal. In concentrating on a current project, it is important not to lose sight of why you undertook it in the first place.

2. Meaning-driven goals. What you do every day should contribute to giving your life meaning. If it doesn't, why are you doing it? The old saying runs: "No one ever got to the end of his life and wished he had spent more time at the office." The time at the office didn't provide any meaning. It wasn't connected to anything larger. It was just work. Meaning in work comes from its connection to the whole of what you want your life to be, not just a piece of it.

3. Inner-directed priorities. People in the Balance Cycle move toward goals *they* have chosen, not their systems' goals. As we have seen, it is often difficult to separate what we want from what our systems want us to want. This is why forming your goals using a structure that is *outside* your systems is so necessary and helpful.

4. Vision-based decision-making. An executive explained how he used his Personal Vision: "It is a template. Whenever an opportunity comes up, I match it up to my Personal Vision. If it will move me toward my Vision, I take it. If not, I politely decline. People often ask me how I can be so decisive and sure about important decisions. The reason is that I know where I'm trying to go, I know why, and I know it with a great deal of clarity and specificity."

People who operate in the Balance Cycle have a positive Personal Vision for the future. They feel that what they do makes the most difference in their ultimate happiness and satisfaction. They see satisfaction in a larger context than immediate gain. They actively seek and find meaning in whatever they do.

People in the Balance Cycle are not surprised by change. In the Stress Cycle, stress, anxiety and depression build to the point of crisis, and the crisis precipitates change. People in the Balance Cycle have already considered what may be next and why. Change becomes part of a whole Personal Vision or plan. People in the Balance Cycle approach Turning Points with a blueprint for making decisions. Above all, they approach Turning Points with the idea of *adding* significantly to their lives, not merely getting rid of things that are causing them stress.

The Balance Cycle may seem like a worthwhile alternative to the Stress Cycle, but how do we get there?

PERSONAL VISION

The vehicle for moving from the Stress Cycle to the Balance Cycle is a Personal Vision for your life and career. A Personal Vision is an image of yourself in a future that is meaningful and fulfilling. It connects you to your own future. It can help you at each Turning Point when you make decisions about your life and career. It can help you *every day* to make those small decisions that add up to the Stress Cycle or the Balance Cycle.

A Personal Vision, though it helps you see into the future, must be absolutely grounded in the present—in you. It must include every significant aspect of who you are and what you want from your life. In the following section, we describe the Personal Vision and explain how to form your own.

THE STRUCTURE OF A PERSONAL VISION

I. A Personal Vision, to be effective, must comprise all important elements of your life and career. It should take into consideration:

> **A. Your stage of adult development.** The Personal Vision of a high school student setting off to college will be different from that of a 42-year-old man who would like to do something different, or a 65-year-old woman planning retirement.
>
> **B. Your natural talents and abilities.** What you naturally do well. Your inborn gifts. If you work against them, work is always labor. If you work with them, everything is easier and more fun.
>
> **C. Your skills and life experience.** What you learn in life creates a hugely valuable asset to take to the next stage of your career. Your Personal Vision should help you use this asset as you grow older and your life changes.
>
> **D. Your interests and fascinations.** What draws your attention, what *pulls* you. From this often-neglected factor springs the source of your most important creative energy.
>
> **E. Your interpersonal style.** Accurately identifying and working through your personal style means that you can work more productively, expend less energy and experience less stress.

F. Your values. What you think is *worth* doing in life. Your values give your life an overall sense of direction and purpose.

G. Your goals. What you want to do in life. What you want to accomplish. Many people find out with a shock that they have been pursuing someone *else's* goals—too late. Figuring out your goals gives you steps to follow, way stations on your path.

H. Your family of origin. Some of the most fundamental concepts you take into adult life developed in the family in which you grew up. Including this in your Personal Vision gives it integrity, depth and meaning, often in profound ways.

II. Your Personal Vision should involve both objective and subjective elements. A Vision must be based on an objective framework. You can assess your natural abilities through objective measurement. Along with your acquired skills and experience, these are the bedrock of your Personal Vision. But the *life* of your Personal Vision depends upon the more subjective factors such as interests, personality, values and goals.

III. It should be based on a structure that is outside of your current work, friend, and family systems. Advice from your family, friends or business associates, however wise and well-meant, can only come from the perspective of your own systems. To gain a more objective and complete view of yourself, you need to step outside your normal systems for a time. This is the only way you can know for sure that your Personal Vision is not just another version of your family's messages, or answers from your current systems.

IV. It should provide a blueprint for important life and career decisions. People who have a Personal Vision are sure of themselves.

THE STRUCTURE OF PERSONAL VISION

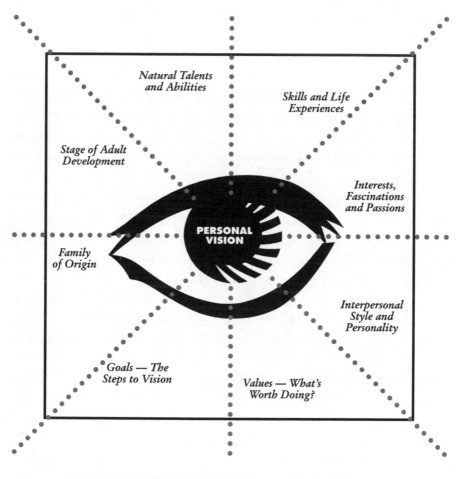

*Natural Talents
and Abilities*

*Skills and Life
Experiences*

*Stage of Adult
Development*

*Interests,
Fascinations
and Passions*

**PERSONAL
VISION**

*Family
of Origin*

*Interpersonal
Style and
Personality*

*Goals — The
Steps to Vision*

*Values — What's
Worth Doing?*

**A PERSONAL VISION, TO BE EFFECTIVE, MUST INCLUDE EIGHT
CRITICAL FACTORS. LEAVE ONE OUT, AND YOU RUN THE
RISK OF FALLING INTO THE STRESS CYCLE.**

At important times, they can act and decide independently of their work and family systems because they have thought through all of the important factors that influence their lives.

Having seen what a Personal Vision is, let's go back to Carol and Jane to see how they developed Personal Visions and moved from the Stress Cycle to the Balance Cycle.

Carol's Story, continued

As you may remember, Carol had reached a point near burnout in her career. She felt her only answer was to quit, and definitely thought she *would* quit within the next two years. As she constructed her Personal Vision, she realized that she was, in many ways, ideally suited for her job. Her abilities were a positive asset, and she loved both the technology involved and the people she dealt with every day. Carol came to realize, however, that she could be a talented teacher. She had been ready to quit her job so that she could go to school, and eventually teach.

When Carol did family-of-origin work, she realized that the powerful messages she had absorbed from her family were still controlling her life. She realized that her company had no interest in changing these patterns, even though one could argue that it would be in the company's interests to help her do so. This would require a long-term focus that systems rarely exhibit. The only way Carol could change would be to take charge of and manage her *own* life and career.

As Carol constructed her Personal Vision, she realized that even though her present company was a great fit for her, significant aspects of her job would need to change. As she got a clearer picture of what she wanted to do, using Surveying, she gradually created a position for herself that would meet her needs and the company's needs, too. In working to create a Personal Vision, she had discovered natural gifts that would help her as a teacher and trainer. Combining these with her desire for a helping role and a schedule that allowed her a personal life, she formed a plan.

She began working with the training department on a consulting basis. She found she was in fact a gifted trainer, and was able to shift more of her responsibilities there. Eighteen months later, she is much more satisfied and has no plans to quit. She feels she is a more valuable asset to the company, because she now trains many others to sell as effectively as she once did.

By getting outside her corporate system, her family system, and her system of friends and colleagues, she was able to come up with a new answer. She could continue to work in the company, but demand more time for a personal life.

Jane's Story, continued

In completing several exercises on values, Jane realized she had a strong wish to do something positive for children in her community. She joined a public-service organization that was devoted to helping young girls at risk stay in school, find jobs and discover new opportunities. She eventually became a board member, and finally ended up being executive director of the board. Her headaches disappeared following one occasion when she insisted that she *was* going to attend an important board meeting over her husband's objections. Her son, perhaps realizing that if his mother could stand up to his father, she would probably take him on next, got off the couch shortly after this, and eventually graduated from college. Her husband doesn't work on Saturday or Sunday any more. This entire family system was transformed by Jane's Personal Vision.

CREATING A PERSONAL VISION

The process of creating a Personal Vision and moving from stress to balance is vital. Nothing is easier than understanding the Stress Cycle, the Balance Cycle and how a Personal Vision can help you move from one to the other. Merely understanding the ideas and grasping the concepts will not accomplish anything as real as the profound changes in Carol's and Jane's lives we described above. Creating a Personal Vision that has the power to change your life must involve all of the following *behavior*:

1. You must **stop**. The Stress Cycle keeps you in constant motion. It keeps your mind constantly occupied. You must give yourself a period of empty time in order to do the work of getting to a Personal Vision. Not 15 minutes when you don't have any other appointments, but significant blocks of time over several weeks or months that are scheduled and inviolable. Chapter Three deals with those natural times of crisis and change in which we are sometimes more open to stopping and looking for alternative answers. Even in the most compelling life crisis, however, nothing will happen unless you decide to stop.

2. You must **get outside of your systems**. Next to stopping, this is the most difficult step. You need answers different from those your family, friends or corporate systems can provide. Not because there is anything wrong with them, but because their stock of answers is virtually identical to your stock of answers. What you need at a Turning Point is the ability to take a fresh look at your answers and preconceptions. This book guides you through a process we developed to help you do this. It takes time and energy, but the payoff can be significant, in terms both of success and of satisfaction. At the end of this chapter and each of the following seven chapters, we

included a series of Thought Experiments. These Thought Experiments provide an action framework to help you create your own Personal Vision.

3. You must engage in a **structured exploration** of all eight critical factors: stage of development, abilities, skills, interests, personality, values, goals and family of origin. If you leave one out, you risk creating a blind spot in your vision that forces you to stumble back into stress and crisis at the next Turning Point. Chapters Three through Seven explain how to explore all of the significant factors involved in a Personal Vision.

4. You need to **integrate creatively** all eight of the significant factors. This task is too complicated to perform logically. How do your values interact with your goals? How do both relate to your natural abilities? These are not linear questions. In order to get to a Personal Vision, you must use your creative mind. Chapter Eight explains creative integration, and the Thought Experiment helps you use your right and left brains to create a Personal Vision.

5. You need to **make it work in the real world**. A Personal Vision that is just an idea is not complete. You need to bring in information from the real world in order to make it a useful tool for your life. In Chapter Nine, we talk about Surveying, an extremely powerful process for translating your vision to real life.

THOUGHT EXPERIMENT A:
A *Personal Vision Notebook*

The Thought Experiments included at the end of this and the next seven chapters are meant to guide you to your own Personal Vision.

Personal Vision Notebook. Buy a spiral-bound notebook of 50 pages or more. You will use this notebook to record and summarize everything you discover in the other Thought Experiments. If you think this sounds like it may involve a lot of writing, you're right. Forcing yourself to write down your discoveries about yourself makes your thoughts, feelings and ideas more usable. Each time you record your findings from Thought Experiments in your notebook, you set the stage for creative and integrative insights. Feel free to sketch or doodle in your notebook, or staple pictures, headlines, advertisements or articles in it. Use it any way that seems helpful to you. But also use it to record your findings about yourself *in words*.

For anyone for whom writing is a particular labor and who feels it would be an unproductive stumbling block, we suggest recording your responses into a tape recorder.

FOUR STORIES OF PEOPLE AT TURNING POINTS
After each Thought Experiment, we will tell continuing stories of four actual people as they proceeded step by step through the program outlined in this book. They will tell you—mostly in their own words—what they discovered from completing the Thought Experiments.

Tracy—23 years old

Tracy graduated from college nine months ago. Since graduating, she has lived at home and worked as a secretary in the law firm of her father's friend. In college, she majored in psychology, intending to earn a Ph.D. and become a psychologist. In her junior year in college she realized that, due to changes in managed care, it was becoming increasingly difficult for psychologists to have satisfying careers or even to earn a living. She gradually gave up her idea of going to graduate school in psychology, but had no alternative plan. When she graduated, she didn't know what to do next. She took the job in the law firm thinking that she could just earn a little money until she could figure out her next step, but nine months later she was no further along than when she started. "Since I graduated, I've been miserable. My parents are supportive, but I know they hate it that I don't seem to be able to bring myself out of this funk. I always did well in school, but this is something I haven't been able to figure out."

How is she feeling at this point? "Depressed. Discouraged. No self-confidence. Cynical about the work world."

Brian and Janet—both 30 years old

Brian works for a major telecommunications company in marketing. He started co-oping there while in college, and was offered a job immediately after graduating. He typically puts in 10- to 11-hour days and works most weekends. He has been married two years to Janet, whom he met at work. "At the end of the day, we are both so exhausted we don't want to cook dinner. We just fix a bowl of cereal and sit and read the paper. Janet wants to have children, but I'm thinking, 'We can't have children yet. I need to get another promotion under my belt.'" Brian looks at the people above him in the hierarchy, and most are just a little older than he is. One or two are younger. He feels that if he doesn't make his mark soon, he will lose his chance and be shuffled aside, or even out.

Brian's feeling now: "I want to get ahead."

Janet has been working in the same company for three years in customer relations. She has never been promoted. "I feel completely unfulfilled at work. I want to be successful there, but I don't like what I'm doing, and I don't really know how to get out of there. What else would I do? What department would I go to? It's confusing. I think if we had a baby, I would just quit and be a mother."

Janet's feeling now: "Tired. Discouraged."

Elizabeth—43 years old

Elizabeth is an executive in a large technology firm. "I work 75-hour weeks. I travel. I never see my child. My husband and I are strangers. There has to be another answer."

Her feeling? "I have to do something. Maybe this will help."

Carl—51 years old

Carl was vice president in Human Resources in a major entertainment company for nine years. Six months ago he was laid off as the result of a merger. This has not been as difficult for him as he thought it might be. "I was ready for a change anyway. This just meant that I have to change now, which, of course, isn't too comfortable. I have no idea whether I should go back into a large company or whether I should try to get a job in a smaller firm. Or maybe start my own consulting business."

His feeling now: "Interested. Hopeful."

NEXT CHAPTER: In the next chapter we begin to move toward a Personal Vision. We start with the adult development cycle—

CHAPTER 3

Crisis and
CHANGE

BOTH SARA, THE YOUNG LAW STUDENT, AND Mitchell, the young person in technology sales whose stories we told in Chapter One, had reached normal adult Turning Points when they realized that stress was taking over their lives and felt something must change. We saw Sara move from high school to college, the first adult Turning Point, and then from college to the work world, the second. At this Turning Point, she wondered if her decisions had been good ones, but saw no way to change. Mitchell, at the Age-30 Turning Point, felt that his career, although a good fit in many ways, still lacked something that he had difficulty articulating. He used the structured process in this book to help him assess and change.

We all face Turning Points during our entire adult working lives, about one every seven to 10 years. They don't even stop with retirement. We continue to have Turning Points every seven to 10 years through our sixties, seventies, eighties and beyond.

Each Turning Point in adult development is initiated by crisis. One sense of "crisis" has a theatrical meaning: the many plot elements of a person's life come together in a decisive peri-od of time. Another sense of "crisis" is a catastrophe. Turning Points have elements of both.

At Turning Points, the strands of our lives unravel slightly, and we decide how to weave them back together. Sometimes at Turning Points, however, we feel as though the entire cable severs, separating our lives into before and after. *In any case, at all Turning Points we make decisions that affect the course of the next seven to 10 years of our lives for better or worse.*

WHAT ARE TURNING POINTS AND HOW DO THEY AFFECT US?

Turning Points, in spite of the name, are not single points in time; they usually spread over one to three years. They signal periods of heightened awareness. At Turning Points people unexpectedly become open to new ideas. They may check out the self-help books in bookstores or the section on Eastern philosophy. Men may become interested in women's maga-zines, or women's issues, or want desperately to connect. A woman might suddenly decide to start a business or have children for the first time. *Both are looking for ways to expand their areas of competence and express themselves more completely.*

Turning Points and crises develop out of the Stress Cycle. As we get further and further into the Stress Cycle, our System Selves become increasingly different from our True Selves. The life we lead no longer expresses who we are, and we become increasingly aware of this fact. We recognize problems in our current lives, and consider alternative solutions. *At all Turning Points we start looking for answers and trying to find some-thing new.*

Unfortunately, at Turning Points most of us don't escape the Lemming Conspiracy. What does a 42-year-old man do when he wakes up one morning to find that he doesn't want to go to work that day? He can't stand the thought of doing what he does all day. This is not an unnatural feeling, nor is it uncommon. A person in this condition may find himself unexpectedly grasping for new answers and seeking new points of view.

A flurry of activity and change may follow. New clothes, new hairstyle or color, new car, new city, new wife, new family. These changes are all on the *outside*. Our 42-year-old in the midst of this flurry may *feel* that each new change expresses the "new him," but unless he has done some serious work on defining the True Self he is trying to express, most of these changes do not lead to any new or creative answers. They just end up throwing him into another round of the Stress Cycle.

Most divorces happen at Turning Points. People also tend to quit jobs or make sudden career moves. This is no accident. People want answers, and they mostly look for these answers in the *externals* of their lives. No creative solution emerges from these approaches. Simple change of externals rarely leads people any closer to their True Selves.

In order to discover answers that can really change life, you must first look *inside*. You have to find out who you really are. Not your System Self, not the you of your family of origin, but your True Self—the self that powerfully wants expression at crises and Turning Points. After you have a clear sense of your True Self from the inside, you can look productively outside for ways to express it.

In Chapter Two, we described how crises develop from the increasing disparity between our System Selves and our True Selves and how this leads to the Stress Cycle. Let us see how the different crises and Turning Points develop over the adult life span.

THE EIGHT TURNING POINTS OF ADULT LIFE

At all Turning Points throughout our adult lives, we must solve the problem of a personal balance between connectedness and productivity. Between being and doing. Love and work. At the earlier Turning Points, we tend to choose one over the other. Our major commitment and energy goes into our family and

THE EIGHT TURNING POINTS OF ADULT LIFE

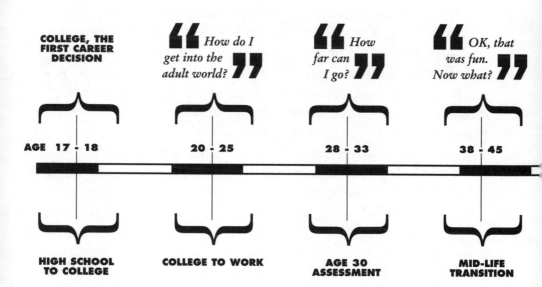

COLLEGE, THE FIRST CAREER DECISION

" How do I get into the adult world? "

" How far can I go? "

" OK, that was fun. Now what? "

AGE 17 - 18   20 - 25   28 - 33   38 - 45

HIGH SCHOOL TO COLLEGE   **COLLEGE TO WORK**   **AGE 30 ASSESSMENT**   **MID-LIFE TRANSITION**

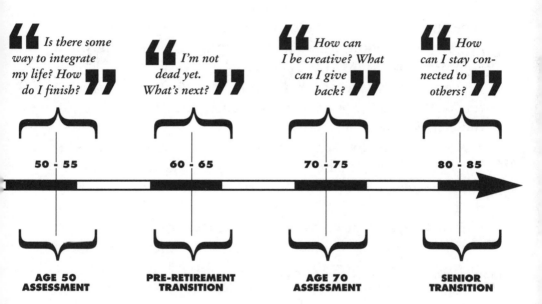

"Is there some way to integrate my life? How do I finish?"

"I'm not dead yet. What's next?"

"How can I be creative? What can I give back?"

"How can I stay connected to others?"

50 - 55   60 - 65   70 - 75   80 - 85

AGE 50 ASSESSMENT   PRE-RETIREMENT TRANSITION   AGE 70 ASSESSMENT   SENIOR TRANSITION marriage, or into work and "making it." Traditionally, in our society, men have gone one way, and women the other. This traditional separation of men's and women's roles is no longer so predictable. When people speak of "having it all," they are referring to this traditional split between work and family; they are saying they want work *and* family. They do not want to make a black-and-white choice, but often they choose in spite of themselves. The wish for both frequently leads to frantic exhaustion in the pursuit of everything.

Balance implies choosing. We each have a limited stock of time and energy—a difficult concept for anyone 30 years old—and we must choose where to invest them. The more fully and completely we know our True Selves, the easier these choices become. At 30, at least for the authors of this book, choosing *less* of this and *more* of that represented heresy. At 40 or 50, these choices seem more reasonable.

After mid-life, lives can become less of an either/or proposition. Men, having made it (or not), may want more intimacy. Some women, perhaps having been intensely involved in family for years, may want to see what they can do out in the world. Other women, having invested their energies in the business world, may suddenly find that they want more intense involvement with a family. In any case, the either/or decision is a blind alley. It doesn't lead to a satisfying long-term resolution. We find that as people mature, as they encounter the Turning Points after mid-life, they are increasingly capable of creating a solution that expresses both balance and choice rather than simply striving for everything. People who achieve this balance seem to have a calm and wisdom from which we can all learn.

Each Turning Point represents a window of time during which we have the energy and drive to examine our former solutions and try again to discover more satisfying ones.

High school to college (17-18 years old): Think back for a moment on how you decided to go to the college you attended.

We know of a young man who went to Princeton. Why? Because it was Princeton. No other reason seemed necessary. Looking back on this important decision, it seems embarrassingly unconsidered to him. Princeton might have been the perfect choice or exactly the wrong one. But without any serious work on what he wanted to do with his life, or what he wanted to get out of college, how could he have possibly known?

Where to go to college is the first career decision most of us make. It begins the crucial process of individuating from our families of origin. We often can't see its importance until we are older and look back, wishing we had explored a different opportunity, or not spent so much time on a dead end. High school seniors and their families typically make this decision with almost no real information about themselves. Most decisions about college are made by some combination of high school grades, SAT scores, teacher recommendations and the reputation of the college. All of these are outside factors; someone else passes judgment on the individual or the school. None of them tell the student anything about his or her *interior*—about such crucial factors as interests, or personality, or natural talents, or goals. Indeed, most students at this age have never considered these interior factors in any detailed way, and have never been encouraged to. Yet their success in college, their success in the adult world, and how much they *enjoy* their lives depend far more on these factors than on grades and SAT scores.

The most important information high school and college students need is an assessment of their natural talents and abilities. But they should also start addressing the "softer" issues too: interests, personality, values and even life goals. These all become increasingly important as we mature, and if students start to get the idea that they are worth paying attention to, it can help them immensely in college and later.

We have talked to some adults who report themselves to be extremely happy with their careers over extended periods of time. They are markedly different from the driven young men and women in their twenties and thirties who are working constantly, have no personal lives, and tell you "Everything's fine!" These adults who have been so satisfied with their work lives always report the same thing: as teenagers, they were positively encouraged by their families to pay attention to and actively follow what they *enjoy*. As a family *value*, the interior experience of what one did was paramount, not the result, or the bottom line. It is also clear that the parents in these families actively demonstrated these values. We cannot stress enough that children absorb the actual values parents *live by*. If these values correspond to what the parents say, then children get a congruent message. If, however, parents live one message and proclaim another, the children always absorb the former. They also learn that what you say does not necessarily need to reflect reality.

High School to College: Two Stories

Ben went to a college-preparatory high school and did well. His grade-point average, SAT scores and teacher recommendations allowed him to enter Cornell University. He was excited about going to his father's alma mater. At Cornell, he enjoyed his classes, but failed to find a peer group with whom he felt compatible. He became increasingly depressed, and when he came home for Christmas break, he decided not to go back.

Ben waited tables for several months after dropping out of college, but also became interested in showing his art. A talented artist, he started an artists' cooperative with two acquaintances.

Ben had never thought about his art in relation to college or to his career. He was indeed academically talented, but obviously there was much more that he could do. He had never considered exactly what he wanted to accomplish in college; it was enough just to go. He had put off thinking about a career altogether.

Patricia, on the other hand, went to college with several ideas in mind. She thought she might like to explore journalism. She was definitely interested in law, and also politics. Patricia deliberately chose a college that offered her the ability to explore all three of her interests.

Patricia worked for the college newspaper for two years, becoming campus editor before deciding that her personality was wrong for newspaper work—she often felt she was forcing herself to capture an interview or a statement in a way that left her dissatisfied and uneasy.

Patricia also worked in her state representative's office for almost a year as part of an internship. She wrote replies to letters from constituents. She enjoyed the feeling of *doing* something, and remained interested in politics. Her law courses really enlivened her, though. She became intensely involved in capital punishment and public interest law.

Patricia graduated from college four years after entering. This put her in a minority. Of her group of seven friends from high school, she was the only one to graduate in four years. She went to law school and is now a practicing lawyer. She remains interested in politics, or perhaps in being a judge someday.

Ben ignored a significant portion of his life when choosing a college. He was never encouraged to think about himself and what he wanted to do with his life. He was never encouraged to think about college as a springboard to his life or to think about how what he did in college might connect to him personally.

Patricia had been encouraged to figure out what she was looking for. The college she chose was not the most prestigious one she was accepted to. It was the one that offered her the clearest opportunity to explore her life.

College to the work world (22 to 25 years old): This is, for many, the final step out of the family home. If successful, a young man or woman leaps into the adult world. If not, he or she falls agonizingly back into the family, and can become dangerously stuck. A recent article in the *New York Times* indicated that almost one in seven males between the ages of 22 and 29 lives at home with his parents.

Many factors conspire to make the transition to the work world more bewildering now than in the past. Although this has always been a difficult step, today there is no clear path. No one joins a large corporation out of college expecting to work there until retirement. Corporations expect young people to be free agents, hired for a finite period to do a particular job. For corporations, the premium is on people who can clearly state their value to the company. Unfortunately this is difficult for anyone who has never examined in any detail just what he or she has to offer an employer.

College students and recent graduates can easily get caught up in externals. The imperative is simple: get a job, any job. What pays the most? What position or industry offers the most security in this era of downsizing? What career fields will capture headlines in the next century? What company provides the best benefits? Is there a secure career track? As important as all of these considerations are, they ignore the central question: *Who am I, and what do I want to do with my life?*

It's no wonder that college students don't typically pay any attention to the question of what to do after college until they are within months of graduating. Job? The work world? It has nothing to do with me.

We talked to hundreds of college students as we researched the ideas in this book. The universal feeling among them is that when they leave college and enter into adult life, they will have to give up most of what they really enjoy about being who they are. They will have to settle down and work hard at a job that is essentially meaningless so they can earn enough money to buy the kinds of things that don't bring their parents much happiness. Many go to graduate school or professional school just so they can put it off a few more years. Who can blame them?

College students need to pay close attention to their natural abilities, but also to their skills. What have they learned in life? How can they use that? Again, their interests, personalities, values and goals should play an important part in gaining a sense of *direction*. Ideally the first job would build upon experiences in college, internships, and summer jobs and be a positive step in a career direction that makes internal sense to the student. Simply joining the firm that sends recruiters to campus can lead to much unhappiness.

College to Work: Emily's Story

Emily majored in marketing at a good college. Her first job was copyediting for a publishing company. She moved from there to a music company and worked at marketing for them, but soon left. While looking for something more to her liking, she took a job as a receptionist at a real estate company. One day she woke up to discover she had been a receptionist at the same company for almost four years. She had never actively pursued anything else. This realization devastated her.

Emily, age 28, went through the program we describe in this book. She discovered that her natural abilities, personality, interests and values all pushed her in the direction of counseling. At her Age-30 Turning Point, she started back to graduate school to earn a degree and eventually a license to practice counseling. The point is that Emily could have known this about herself at any time—before college, during college, after college. By expending concentrated effort and attention to figure this out, she could have made better use of her time in college, worked in jobs that expanded her horizons and helped her career ambitions, and focused her energy on graduate school earlier instead of trying desperately to make it in jobs that weren't rewarding to her. She didn't need to waste so much of her time—and feel so badly about herself for so long.

Age-30 Assessment (28 to 33 years old): This Turning Point typically happens between the ages of 28 and 33. Regardless of the direction in which we launch ourselves in our early twenties, we do some reassessment around age 30. If we jumped right out of college into a job and started working like crazy, by this time we begin asking some predictable questions. Is this getting me what I want? Could I see myself doing this for another 10 years? How far can I go with this company? What else should I be doing? Should I make a move to get myself on the fast track? If our jobs seem to be getting us what we want, we start asking about lifestyles. Shouldn't I get a new car? Maybe it's time to get married. Maybe it's time to have a baby.

People always make *some* decision at this age. Just as with earlier Turning Points, most people look to the outside for their answers. The answer to the discomfort of the Stress Cycle is a new car, or marriage, or a child, or a new job, or a promotion. *They almost never start by asking themselves who they are and what they would really like to be doing in the first place.* The significant questions at this age are more like these: "Is this what I want to be doing? What doesn't fit? If my career keeps going in the same way it is now, where will I be in 10 years? Is that where I want to be? Why? What do I want to add to my life to make it fuller?"

At this Turning Point, the main issues revolve around goals. What do I really want in life? Is what I am doing going to get me that? If not, I need to do something different. If so, what else should I be shooting for? People who have been paying attention all along to the softer, interior issues like interests and values are in a much better position to use the creative energy of this Turning Point to position themselves in a career they will actively enjoy over the next 10 years or so.

The majority have not been paying attention. A great many young people get started in jobs in their early twenties that will not be able to take them anywhere. How many young college graduates or dropouts do you know who are waiting tables or working at some other dead-end job? They are (perhaps) able to support themselves in an apartment, pay for gas, and pay for their entertainment. At the Age-30 Assessment, it suddenly dawns on them that their lives will not take them anywhere. They can't get married, can't have a family, can't have anything like the life of their parents if they continue. Often young people at this age start over. They might go to school or become serious about finding a job with a future. We saw this pattern in Emily's story above.

The other main group consists of the young people who have started in a career or a profession and at this Turning Point start to get serious about it. It's not fun any more. If they are going to get to the top, they have to do it *now*. The top, of course, is one of the fundamentally subversive myths of the Lemming Conspiracy. The top is understood without question or comment to be a positive goal and unquestionably worth achieving. Like all myths, it imparts a message about values and the way one should live. But it is a dangerous myth because it never addresses the interior of the person.

Regardless of how well or poorly people make decisions at the Age-30 Assessment, they move into their thirties and a period of stability. They may be miserable and hate their jobs, but they don't change course during these years. Even if the thirties are productive and satisfying, people inevitably come to Mid-Life, a time of change, transition and starting over—especially for men.

Age-30 Assessment: Paul and Melinda's Story

Paul and Melinda both worked in large corporations, Paul as a manager in a technology company, Melinda as an accountant in a large international accounting firm. Married at 25, both were now in their early thirties. Both Paul and Melinda sensed that time was running out. Melinda felt that, if she were going to have children, it must be now. Paul felt that he had to get on the fast track in his company in the next two years, or he would never make it as far as he wanted to go.

They decided to have children, and their first was born when they were both 32. Another child followed a year later. Paul enrolled in an executive M.B.A. program; in addition, he asked for, and got, extra projects from his boss. Melinda was offered a promotion, but she would have had to move overseas, so she decided not to take it. They had money for the first time in their marriage; they moved into a new house and bought nice cars. They hired a nanny. Melinda was offered another promotion that required moving to another city. She felt she would have to take this promotion or see her career evaporate. Paul put in for a transfer to a city near the one where Melinda and the two children would be, but he felt this would definitely be a backwards career move for him. His boss was now actively interested in him and promoted his cause in the company. The new city would not have the kind of visibility as he had now. Paul already felt some resentment about being asked to make this choice.

The last thing either Paul or Melinda wanted to hear was that they should take a few weeks to sort through their lives and figure out what they really wanted. The Stress Cycle gripped both. Although each had goals, and they each expended a great deal of energy toward attaining them, neither felt centered. They tried to pursue everything society and their families had laid out for them to do, but never stopped to figure out what would be meaningful to them.

Both Paul and Melinda made significant career moves and decisions during this Turning Point. Neither, however, dealt with limits. They wanted marriage *and* children *and* expensive things *and* career advancement *and* success *and* recognition. (How far? How much? "As far as possible" and "Everything" were their only answers.) They didn't *want* to choose between these goals.

By age 34, they were trying to maintain a marriage at a distance. Paul decided not to move so that he could continue working with his boss. His ambition had settled on moving into the executive ranks. Melinda was being offered steady advancement in her firm, but this entailed a great deal of travel. They earned enough to have a full-time nanny who took care of the children. By their mid-thirties, Paul and Melinda had grown far apart. They seemed to be waiting for a signal that it was time to divorce.

Eventually they will be brought up short. Paul may get downsized. Melinda might have an affair. One of their children might develop problems at school. They might get divorced. Any or all of these life events tell us one thing: "You have to stop." It sometimes happens at the Mid-Life Transition.

The Mid-Life Transition (38 to 45 years old): The Mid-Life Transition can be one of the most important and significant events in many people's lives. Or it can be an unmitigated disaster. It is no coincidence, certainly, that people in their early forties in the midst of mid-life turmoil often have teenage children who are in the midst of the turmoil of leaving home. The parents and the teenagers are trying to solve the same problem. They both seek to create or recreate themselves so that they can function in the adult world.

Our society is used to thinking of Mid-Life as a crisis, in the sense of a catastrophe. Mid-Life is really no more important than any of the other Turning Points. It may be just the first time many people become aware of any change in their lives. It is a catastrophe for many because they have ignored their True Selves for many years, accepting systems' answers for who they are and what they should be doing. Eventually, most people become aware of the disparity between the person they feel themselves to be and the person through whom they function, their System Selves. When the disparity is large and the effort to keep it hidden from awareness is overwhelming, the realization can be sudden and intense. It can lead people to seek sudden and catastrophic answers.

Stories are legion. People at Mid-Life have affairs. They get divorced. They suddenly derail from the fast track. They get depressed; they take Prozac. Men want to buy a sports car. Women want to have surgery. They may want to start their own businesses. They may want to change jobs. It's exciting. It's crazy.

It's scary. One of the worst outcomes of Mid-Life is nothing. Many people, confronted with feelings of stress, anxiety and depression, choose to ignore them. It's too frightening. To open the door to change is to release demons, lose control over them forever. Better to simply endure.

In the short term, this strategy of perseverance appears successful. The upsetting feelings of Mid-Life go away. People settle down to the life they were living before. But the feelings haven't really gone away; they have just gone underground. The True Self still needs expression. People who just endure have only given themselves a short reprieve. They often find that when the feelings of upset come back at the next Turning Point, they are much more intense and overwhelming. And solutions are correspondingly more catastrophic.

The main issues at Mid-Life revolve around *values*. Usually, we know how far we can go in our careers by the end of the thirties. We know whether or not we can get to the top. We have a sense of how much income we can expect to bring in. We have a sense of what we can accomplish. We also turn an invisible corner sometime around age 40; half our lives are over. So a question begins to impose: Does what I am doing seem *worth* doing?

This is life's great question; wrestling with it makes us grow and figure out what we want. Too many people confront it, though, and try to forget about it. There doesn't seem to be any ready answer. Change feels unthinkable. And how do you figure out what's worth doing anyway?

It becomes increasingly important as you get older to feel that what you are doing is meaningful. What makes work meaningful is different for everyone, but too many people don't consider this question important. They feel that being an adult means holding down a job and providing for a family. Often at Mid-Life they are surprised by feelings that their lives aren't enough. What's missing is the interior—the True Self.

Mid-Life Transition: Steven's Story

Steven, age 44, was married with three children. The oldest was 15. He had been married 20 years. He had worked in banking since he graduated from college. He had been with the same bank for 13 years and was the manager of a department in the home office. One morning he read in the paper that his bank had been acquired by a larger bank in a complicated merger.

Within six months he was laid off because of the merger and restructuring of the two organizations. He had six months of severance pay and a good outplacement package. In the outplacement counseling, he was told that anger and depression were common reactions to his situation, but that the best answer was to dust himself off and get right back out there. Clearly the best way to jump back "out there" would be to land another job in banking.

Steven was suddenly acutely aware of his life and career balancing delicately between two paths, and that now he must choose. He could return to banking, a world he knew, or he could strike out in a different direction.

Steven chose to go through a program like the one presented in this book. He sorted through what made his life valuable and meaningful to him, and what seemed beside the point. In a practical sense, he knew he needed to capitalize on his banking knowledge, contacts, and background. But in an emotional sense, he realized he would rather sell hot dogs than work for another banking conglomerate. In his program he discovered natural talents in sales and strategic marketing that had never been evident to him. He had long held that his family came first, and he determined that anything he did would not compromise that value.

Steven ended up making a proposal to a smaller firm that outsources human resource services to large firms, such as banks. His contacts and experience in the banking world make him quite knowledgeable when talking to potential customers. He does not get paid as much as he made before, but he feels much more control of his life. Learning a new job and a new field has been very exciting. "I feel that I have gotten to try a whole new life, and I like it! I like the entrepreneurial feel of the company, and I like it that some days I go to work and I'm just making it up, because no one has tried what I'm doing before. I love that feeling."

Age-50 Assessment (50 to 55 years old): You may notice that throughout the adult developmental cycle, the questions become increasingly complex and subjective. The Age-50 Assessment, just like the Age-30 Assessment, is a Turning Point in which we reassess the answers of the previous Turning Point. If those answers were grossly inappropriate, such as quitting basically productive jobs and rewarding marriages, we may start over at this Turning Point. If we did nothing at Mid-Life, if we just had the feelings and simply endured, then the anxiety and depression of Mid-Life come back in spades. If our solutions at Mid-Life really brought the way we live closer to an expression of our True Selves, we may make small course corrections at this Turning Point.

By the Age-50 Assessment, it is impossible to pin down a single issue that is more important than the others. Living a life that feels meaningful is the only real way to come to terms with the end of life. The alternative to meaning is despair.

Just as the Mid-Life Transition is particularly powerful for men, the Age-50 Assessment appears to have particular meaning and potency for women. In fact, some evidence indicates that, for women, the true Mid-Life Transition may not be at 40, but at 50. Whereas men who have been trying to make it in the world suddenly at age 40 feel their isolation and begin grasping for connection, women who have connected all along by age 50 are seeing many of those relationships change and disappear. Children leave home and start lives of their own. Parents die. Husbands divorce. It is at this age that women's bodies say clearly: "Childbearing is over."

Many women whose focus has always been toward family and connection find that they move *outward* at this age, in the opposite direction from men. Now they want to see what they can *do* in the world. They want to make an impact. Women who have had successful careers may find themselves, like men at this age, wanting to make some changes to bring more balance to their lives.

Both men and women must find a different way to communicate inside their families. If they don't, and many do not, they run the significant risk of isolation. Children, now adults, no longer need their constant time, energy and attention. Husbands and wives must find a new basis for their relationship. Many men, in an effort to create the intimacy they missed in first families, start new families. Many women look for a new "baby" to nurture—a business, a cause or a lover.

Both men and women need fuller lives at this age. Both need to achieve a balance between being and doing, relating and producing. Change is inevitable here, and just like at Mid-Life, often catastrophic "solutions" like divorce are nothing more than attempts to deny and ignore change. Ideally, couples at this Turning Point can discover a partnership between equals. Once they have gotten over the fact that things are different, they can go on to figure out that *they* are different and they have many more options to create different relationships.

By this age our lives are the accumulation of all of our choices and decisions. It is difficult to take back earlier choices that limited us or kept us from expression of our True Selves, or kept us from even knowing who our True Selves were. But any choice we make at this Turning Point to help us know who we really are can open doors to express our True Selves.

Age-50 Assessment: Marjorie and Wade

When Wade was 52, his company asked him to take over a division in New York. It would mean a higher profile, being closer to the decision-makers at the home office. He refused. He did not want to move to the Northeast. He did not want to uproot his family. He did not want a more pressurized life. He knew his position in the company was secure, but that this decision would take him off of the fast track he had been on for much of his career.

Wade realized that he and his wife were virtual strangers after years of raising children and maintaining two careers. He also realized that, unless he did something, they would stay that way. He took some vacation time and he and his wife spent almost a month on a walking tour of England and Wales. It was the best time he and his wife have had together since they were dating.

Marjorie, 53, was a successful counselor. She had been single for years and her children were now grown and out of the house. She enjoyed her counseling practice, perhaps more now than she had in years. She no longer felt so stressed by her clients. She liked them more and felt more warmth toward them. She had cut back her hours a little the previous year, and now cut them back again. She felt financially secure, although she was not wealthy.

At 50, Marjorie had started art lessons. As a child and young adult, she painted a great deal, but marriage, children, a career and divorce had drained her energy for it. Now she threw herself into art with great enthusiasm. She tried different media and experimented with different styles. She put her art in her office and home. She loves having her art around her. She has a network of friends who are artists also, some younger, some older. She finds this association with a whole different set of people from her academic and counseling friends very rewarding.

Marjorie does not think she will ever retire completely from counseling; however, she plans to cut back her hours even more, spend more time with art and perhaps travel a little with friends.

Pre-Retirement Transition (60 to 65 years old): Just like the transition from the family to the adult world in our twenties and the Mid-Life transition of our forties, at this transition, we again create a new life. The biggest mistake is ignoring the issue, assuming that retirement means the absence of work. Or assuming that if you have planned financially for retirement, that's all the planning you need to do.

Far from being a time of idyllic rest, retirement for many is a time of aimlessness and emptiness. People die from lack of meaning. If you don't believe that, look at statistics for death by suicide among senior citizens. But suicide isn't necessary. When people feel no purpose to their lives, they tend to get sick and die within just a year or two.

By this age, a fact of all lives is *loss*. We lose parents, spouses, friends, relatives, school chums, even children. We may stop working, and that is a loss. Our bodies may change; we become visibly older. We lose the strength, health and potency of middle age. We creep into the region inhabited by old people.

The most productive answers at all Turning Points *add* to life. They supply some important element we have missed until now. This general rule becomes even more critical as we grow older, when it is often so tempting to give in to loss.

The Pre-Retirement Transition sets the stage for one of the major movements of life. According to demographic statistics, people who live healthily to this age will probably live past 80. This means that at this Turning Point you are preparing for a period of over 20 years. This significant span of years can be mainly marked by emptiness, loss and meaninglessness, or defined by connection, meaning and productivity. The difference between one and the other relates directly to the quality of one's Personal Vision.

Ideally, the Pre-Retirement Transition, like all of the other Turning Points, should build on everything that has gone before. It should be an expression of all a person has learned, believed in, wanted to accomplish and *is*. But it should also be *new*. People looking at retirement should be thinking about what they want to continue doing in retirement, what they want to drop, and what they want to add. They should be creating a Personal Vision for how their lives in retirement will be, what will be meaningful for them.

Generally, this is not something that a person should tackle after he or she has already retired. We feel that the process of thinking and planning for a life of retirement should begin at least five years before. (Clearly, this is true of the other Turning Points, too. As people become more aware of the regularity of change at mid-life, we may find that they become more proactive about planning changes in their careers to make them less catastrophic and more productive.) The questions that are important have to do with summing up a life. What do I want to leave the world? What will be my legacy to the world for having been here? How will the next 20 years contribute to that legacy?

Having a Personal Vision at this age that answers these kinds of questions undoubtedly helps people live longer. But it also helps them live better, more fully, with more satisfaction. If you see those rare senior citizens who are vital, active, and alert into their nineties, they have a Personal Vision. They have a reason to live and a purpose for pushing ahead. A Personal Vision can save your life.

Pre-Retirement Transition: Tom's Story

At age 60, Tom's company asked him to take a retirement package. He had a comfortable income from investments, a home that was paid for, and a wife of 10 years who was 12 years younger than he. She was a physician with a successful practice.

Tom had always known he would retire, but had never thought about what he would *do*. He was happy to be away from his company, but was angry about being shoved out. About a month after retiring, he decided to take up woodworking. He bought several expensive power tools and had some workmen come in to transform some unused basement space into a shop. He hovered over them as they worked, constantly criticizing their work. Several carpenters quit before the job was done. When the shop was finished and the tools installed, Tom had no idea what to make. He thought he would make some toys for his grandchildren, but became frustrated with several elaborate projects before they were done.

Tom became increasingly morose and isolated. Calling a former business associate to have lunch with him was intensely humiliating. The former business associate could not figure out why Tom was calling him, and he didn't have a free lunch date open for weeks. "But let's stay in touch. Say, Tom, sorry, I have another call coming in. Let's talk soon." Tom started watching soap operas during the day. At night he talked about their plots with his wife.

Six months into retirement, Tom's wife knew he was clinically depressed. She was actually the catalyst for change: "If you don't figure out what to do with your life, I'm going to divorce you. Period." He went through the structured program we describe in this book. It was clear he was not ready to retire, and that he would be much happier working for a while longer. He took some consulting work in his old industry—enough to feel creative and productive. He and his wife plan to retire together in 10 years or so.

Age-70 Assessment (70 to 75 years old): The most important career questions at this age have to do with what you can give back to the world. By this age, you have a huge stock of knowledge and experience, but what can you do with it? All of us need to feel connected with others. In the same way, we also need to feel we are productive. This doesn't mean holding down a high-powered job, or earning mountains of money. We can feel productive if we are able to pass on our experience to a younger generation and help that generation grow and thrive.

Having a Personal Vision for these years can make the difference between living and dying, both emotionally and physically. We all need a purpose—a reason to get up in the morning and keep breathing. We all have this purpose inside, if we can identify it and articulate it.

This Turning Point gives us a chance to assess and correct decisions we made earlier. Change comes rapidly during this period of our lives. Our bodies change, our friends' bodies change. People close to us die. If we have not accepted retirement, it is often forced upon us. People tend to separate into three groups by this age:

■ The majority who settle down, become less active physically and mentally, and create familiar lives close to friends and family.

■ A large minority who become increasingly isolated by distance, illness, poverty, death of significant others, and/or gradual personality change.

■ A small minority who shift their activities into new arenas, but who remain physically and mentally vital. They do not release their holds on life, but seem intent on returning gifts from long and productive lives to the community as a whole. Jimmy and Rosalynn Carter, as well as Paul Newman and Joanne Woodward and many other public figures, exemplify this kind of choice.

Age-70 Assessment: Robert's Story

For 35 years, Robert was the principal of a high school. He retired at 60. At this time, his wife became ill with bone cancer, and he cared for her full-time for the next eight years until she died. Robert maintained a wide circle of friends in the small town where he lived. Many people there had been his students in high school; others had been friends since they and Robert were in school together.

Three years after his wife died, Robert met a woman slightly older than he who had been married to a well-known physician for many years. He had died of a heart attack the previous year. Robert and this woman began seeing each other regularly, having dinner together almost every night. They started dance lessons, and went dancing most weekends. They then started a dance group among their friends. Every few months they traveled—sometimes with a group to Europe or Asia, sometimes to see their children and grandchildren. Robert maintained a large garden and became an accomplished grower of roses. He volunteered his time with a neighborhood youth program and at the senior citizen center. He feels healthy and alive; he feels his life is busy and that what he does means something to others who are important to him.

Senior (Age-80) Transition (80 to 85 years old): Change continues. Here change involves the gradual shift from independence to increased dependence. Now your Personal Vision must help you make the utterly creative leap toward connection and productivity while dealing with appropriate dependence. Above all, one must achieve a working balance—remember, this means *choosing*—between appropriate dependence and remaining a vital actor in one's own life.

It may be easy to ignore the fact that this transition is just as important and may shape just as much of your life as the other major transitions of your life. People who reach this transition and are healthy may be making decisions about the next 10 or 20 years of their lives. This is why it is so important to make plans and be proactive about keeping alive mentally and physically.

It is too easy to make King Lear's mistake. Lear decided he had graduated in life to the point that he should be taken care of, rather than take care of himself. He had accomplished much, given his children much, and now he wanted to reap his reward of rest and passivity. The result was disaster, of course.

Lear wanted to abdicate the role of actor of his own life. He felt he *deserved* to be cared for as he wished, without participating in that care.

This time in life can be an opportunity to *be*, certainly, to accept oneself and one's life as it is. We often see people of this age who are able to use their lives' balance and stability to give—not money, but a sense of reinforcement and reward to a younger generation.

WHY REAL CHANGE RARELY HAPPENS

As we have seen, each of the adult Turning Points is brought on by the Stress Cycle, the disparity between our Systems Selves and our True Selves, and the sense of crisis this engenders. We want change; our old answers are not working well; we are stressed. At these times we seek a better expression of our True Selves.

But rarely is anyone able to get outside of systems during these periods of openness and change. As we have seen, corporate and school systems cannot help anyone discover anything about True Selves. The System Self is all any system can deal with. Most of our "spontaneous" answers at Turning Points actually come out of our families of origin. As we have seen with Mitchell's story and Sara's story, we will invariably use the same kinds of solutions for about the same reasons as one or the other of our parents used at the same Turning Point.

There are three common outcomes at Turning Points:

Endure. Ignore your feelings of stress and anxiety, tell yourself to grow up, and keep on doing what you are doing. As we have seen above, this effectively puts off the issue of change for five to seven years, but sets up an even more catastrophic change at the next Turning Point.

Appear to change. Many people, when confronted with the wish for change, do not know what to do with it. Systems urge us to pay attention to the outside, not to our interiors. A new car can be wonderful, but it won't make your life meaningful. Neither will a new job, unless it is connected to a Personal Vision. Even with a drastic change such as divorce, people usually find that the same issues of stress, anger, anxiety and depression come back. These external changes can't bring your True Self and your System Self any closer together.

Actually change. This is a rare outcome. It is always the result of getting *outside* systems and doing structured work on who you are and what you really want from your life. You have to sort out the messages from your family of origin that may be perfect for you from those that may not fit any more.

Real change usually involves *adding* to your life. It is almost never a product of simply removing something.

With real change, your first goal is to figure out how your System Self and True Self have diverged, but ultimately the goal is to find the best expression of your True Self. This may involve giving up some aspects of your job or personal life that do not fit any more. But this is never enough. You must *add* something to your life that is missing.

Real change is virtually impossible to accomplish alone. Any answer you discover on your own will probably be one derived from your systems: your spouse, your friends, your company, your church, your lover. They know you too well. They are all part of your systems. The answers we get from systems may feel real and obvious, but they don't lead to any real change at Turning Points.

Richard's Story

Richard, age 41, was a veteran 20-year insurance executive. He had worked for the same large international company since he graduated from college. On the fast track, he was definitely heading toward the top. He was well-liked by his boss and known to the management of the company.

"I sat at my desk with the door closed one day, going over my options. The only thing I could think to do was to quit. It seemed like the only option that made sense. My boss and my friends at the company would have been more than surprised if they had known where my thinking had led me that day. None of them had any idea about these feelings, but they had become increasingly apparent and important to me."

Richard was at the Mid-Life Turning Point. His feelings were normal and made sense in a larger context. But they didn't make sense to him at the time. He could not articulate exactly what made continued work for his company impossible. He knew he was just as productive as ever, but it wasn't fun any more. He loved his wife and kids, and his job allowed him time and energy to be with them. But he didn't feel any *challenge* to life.

Instead of quitting, Richard "embarked on a quest." He read everything he could about change at mid-career and talked to all of his friends about what they were feeling. He found out that some level of discontent at his age is not only not unusual, but in reality is the overwhelming norm—for both men and women.

THE STEPS TO CHANGE

What is real change, and how does it happen? Richard, in the story above, didn't need a simple answer or new motivational talk. He also didn't need the answers coming from his systems: "Don't be a fool. Just keep doing what you're doing, and you will be set for life." "You've got a good job with a good paycheck, a family to raise, and good prospects for the future. Don't rock the boat." These, or their variants, are the system's answer to Richard's dilemma.

In order for Richard to discover his own answers, he must first *get outside the system*. He must escape the Lemming

Conspiracy. In the course of his research, Richard found a structured process to look systematically at each factor of his career. This process was independent of his systems and its goals were fundamentally different from those of his company, his family, even his friends.

Systems kept Richard from really looking at himself and what he wanted. They asked him to focus on *results*, on the outside, his position, his possessions, his responsibilities. They did not, nor could they, ask him to focus on Richard. In order to beat the Lemming Conspiracy, Richard would need *new information*. He would need information that was not in his systems and that he didn't yet know about himself.

It turned out that one of the most crucial pieces of information Richard needed was about his natural talents and abilities—those inborn characteristics that make it easy to do some kinds of tasks, and difficult to do others. Richard found out that he had a natural problem-solving ability we call Classification. (We will talk about Classification in detail in Chapter Four.) He knew how he liked to tackle problems, but he had not known what a powerful impact this strong ability had on his work life. It drove him to despair when he didn't use it every day. As he looked forward to a comfortable life in the insurance industry, there was no outlet for his ability to solve new problems and deal with rapid change.

In the next chapter, we will talk about abilities in detail, specifically about the powerful Driving Abilities that shape so much of what roles we are particularly suited for, and what ones we are not.

Richard had known he wasn't happy. But he thought he should just grow up, buckle down, and do his job. The *new information* he now had was that, objectively, his job would not make use of his most powerful and insistent ability. He could make a completely effective case to his boss, and his wife, because he had gotten information from outside the systems and had used this information to create a Personal Vision. We will see more of what happened with Richard in Chapter Five.

A STRUCTURED PROCESS TO ESCAPE SYSTEMS

One of the most difficult aspects of gaining your own Personal Vision is sidestepping the Lemming Conspiracy—getting outside your own systems. We have found that the most effective strategy for defeating the Lemming Conspiracy is following a *structured process*. The process we developed includes *all* of the factors a person needs to consider at life Turning Points. Following a structure insures that you systematically take into account not only factors that are comfortable to you, but also ones that you might not think about otherwise. If you only include factors in your Personal Vision that feel "right" to you, or that you would think of yourself, you will only follow your own system. On the other hand, if you follow an external structure for creating your Personal Vision, the structure itself will force you to pay attention to what is important, whether it feels "right" in your system or not. This chapter and the next five chapters detail the structure we researched, developed, tested, and have used with our clients.

GETTING OUTSIDE OF SYSTEMS—HARDER THAN IT MAY APPEAR

Your friends, your family, your colleagues, your boss, your relatives, your fellow church, synagogue or club members—they are all part of the Lemming Conspiracy. In spite of their most loving intentions, they are connected to you in a way that makes it impossible for them to help you gain a new perspective on your life. Basically, all they can do is help you keep doing what you have always been doing. Even if you change jobs, change cities, or change marriages, you always eventually wind up stuck in the same place you have always been *unless you escape your systems*.

ESCAPING YOUR SYSTEMS: A PRIMER

We have discovered several factors that help people escape, briefly, the boundaries of their systems in order to see a wider picture.

One of the most difficult aspects of gaining a Personal Vision is *stopping*—setting aside a significant amount of time and energy to do the work. As we have seen, the Stress Cycle makes stopping seem impossible. The Stress Cycle makes it appear that everything is urgent and nothing can be put aside for a time so that you can figure out how you want to live your life.

The structured process we developed and describe in this book will help you get to all of the important factors you need to consider at the Turning Points of your adult life. It is thorough and effective. We did not create it to be a Band-Aid or motivational trick to excite you for a while, but lead nowhere. It is a process to use *now*, and at any future Turning Point, to help you envision the next stage of your life.

Doing the work of articulating each of the eight critical factors and then integrating them into a Personal Vision is not something you can do in a day, or even a weekend. You need to give your creative mind and logical mind a chance to work on the problem of getting to a Vision over a period of several weeks or months. As you tackle this work, you will find that you may labor over a problem—how to integrate values and goals, for instance—only to be frustrated in coming up empty-handed. A week later, you may be surprised to find you *have* an answer, waiting for you. Your unconscious mind worked on the problem while you had been thinking consciously about something else. The structured process we developed makes conscious use of your creative mind. For the kind of problems we deal with— how to live your life fully and with enthusiasm—it is the most powerful part of your brain, by far. You will find that the Thought Experiments use your logical mind *and* your creative mind. You'll need both to create a transforming Personal Vision.

THOUGHT EXPERIMENT B:
Your Developmental Time Line

In your Personal Vision notebook, make a page for each Turning Point of your life from the first one, High School to College, through the Senior Transition.

1. High School to College (age 17-18)
2. College to Work (age 22-25)
3. Age-30 Assessment (age 28-33)
4. Mid-Life Transition (age 38-45)
5. Age-50 Assessment (age 50-55)
6. Pre-Retirement Transition (age 60-65)
7. Age-70 Assessment (age 70-75)
8. Senior Transition (age 80-85)

Write about the answers to the questions below in your notebook. But *don't* write about them in past tense as though you are your age looking back; write in present as though you are looking forward. For instance, you would write, "I plan to be a doctor, but I am not sure, because I'm afraid it could turn out to be fairly boring. I just don't know what else to look at." Write either from your *actual* point of view at 18 or from the point of view of yourself as 18, but incorporating all that you have learned since then.

Proceed to each Turning Point, writing in each *as though you were that age*. Go backwards to all previous Turning Points. Do your present (or next) Turning Point. Go forward to all future Turning Points. Use the questions to get started, but write about anything that seems significant in how you were assessing your life at the time (or imagine yourself assessing it in the future) and in making plans for the next section of your life.

HIGH SCHOOL TO COLLEGE (AGE 17-18)

Answer these questions as though you were 18. What are the main issues on your mind? What are the main decisions you are facing? What relationships are about to change (e.g., between you and your parents, or you and your high school friends)? In looking to the future, what are the most important factors you are thinking about? What are your plans for the future? Why? What plans do you have for your career? Why? How did you choose that direction among all the possible directions you could have chosen? What are your main talents? What dreams do you have about the kind of life you want? Why?

COLLEGE TO WORK (AGE 22-25)

What skills have I developed? What experience do I have? What kind of work am I most interested in? In choosing a career path, what is the most important deciding factor? What kind of lifestyle do I want? Is what I am doing leading me to that kind of lifestyle?

AGE-30 ASSESSMENT (AGE 28-33)

What has been working about the course I chose? What hasn't been working? What do I want to achieve in the next 10 years? How will I do that? What would I need to change to put myself in a better position? What do I want my life to be like 10 years from now? What values do I need to pay attention to? What interests? What are my family goals? How am I balancing work and family? What would be most meaningful to me at this point in my career? What could I *add* to my life to make it more interesting and meaningful?

MID-LIFE TRANSITION (AGE 38-45)

How do I feel about my family? How do I feel about work? What changes would I like to make in the balance of work and family? How connected do I feel to others? What excites me about work? What has become old and stale? What else besides work would I find exciting? Or, what new direction in my life would feel interesting and fascinating to me? What could I pursue that would be interesting and meaningful? What values do I need to pay attention to? How could I carry that out? What goals do I have for the next 20 years of my career? What needs to happen to accomplish them? What experience and what skills of the first 20 years of my career do I want to be sure to take with me into the next?

AGE-50 ASSESSMENT (AGE 50-55)

Note for women: Many of the questions of the previous section on Mid-Life may apply to you at this Turning Point.

What has been working about the course I chose? What hasn't been working? What do I want to achieve in the next 10 years? How will I do that? What would I need to change to put myself in better position? What do I want my life to be like 10 years from now? What values do I need to pay attention to? What interests? What are my family goals? How am I balancing work and family? Is what I am doing meaningful? If not, why not? How could I make my career more meaningful? What could I *add* to my life to make it more interesting and meaningful?

PRE-RETIREMENT TRANSITION (AGE 60-65)

How do I feel about my family? How do I feel about work?

What changes would I like to make in the balance of work and family? How connected do I feel to others? What excites me about work? What has become old and stale? What else besides work would I find exciting? Or, what new direction in my life would feel interesting and fascinating to me? What could I pursue that would be interesting and meaningful? What values do I need to pay attention to? How could I carry that out? What goals do I have for the next 20 years of my career? What needs to happen to accomplish them? What experience and what skills of the first 40 years of my career do I want to be sure to take with me into the next phase? What could I give back to the world? How could I do that? Who could benefit from my knowledge and experience?

AGE-70 ASSESSMENT (AGE 70-75)

What losses am I contending with? What losses can I expect in the next 10 years? How can I provide enough reinforcement in life to keep me healthy and happy? What has been working about the course I chose? What hasn't been working? What do I want to achieve in the next 10 years? How will I do that? What would I need to change to put myself in better position? What do I want my life to be like 10 years from now? What values do I need to pay attention to? What interests? What are my family goals? How am I balancing work and family? Is what I am doing meaningful? If not, why not? How could I make my career more meaningful? What could I *add* to my life to make it more interesting and meaningful?

SENIOR TRANSITION (AGE 80-85)

What losses am I contending with? What losses can I expect in the next 10 years? How can I provide enough reinforcement in life to keep me healthy and happy? How do I feel about my family? How do I feel about my day-to-day life? What changes would I like to make in the balance of activity and family? How connected do I feel to others? What excites me about my daily life? What has become old and stale? What other kind of activity would I find exciting? Or, what new direction in my life would feel interesting and fascinating to me? What could I pursue that would be interesting and meaningful? What values do I need to pay attention to? How could I carry that out? What goals do I have for the next 10 years of my life? What needs to happen to accomplish them? What experience and what skills of my working life do I want to be sure to take with me into the next phase? What could I give back to the world? How could I do that? Who could benefit from my knowledge and experience? What forum or group could use my experience?

Wait for a few days, and then read over everything you have written about Turning Points. Do you see any recurring themes? What issues keep coming up? What new issues come up, and at what ages? What were the key decisions you made in your life? How did you make them? Were you always aware of what the impact of key decisions would be, or not? What key decisions can you see in the future?

FOUR STORIES: TURNING POINTS

Tracy

"At 18, I didn't know what I wanted to do; I just picked the best college I could get into. I guess I had always assumed I would be a doctor, but I didn't want to be as driven as my father, who is a doctor. The only kind of life I could imagine would be some kind of professional. I'm at a Turning Point now, and I still want to be some kind of professional; I'm just confused about how to do it. I imagine the future being just about like the lives of my father and mother. I'm a doctor or lawyer or something; I work all the time. I pull in a good income. I help people."

Feelings now: "I'm surprised at how hard this was. I'm also surprised at how the only thing I can really picture is my parents' lives. My main feeling is, 'How dull.'"

Brian and Janet

Brian: "When I was 18, I knew I wanted to go into business. I chose a college that had a good business school with a strong marketing department. My vision at the time was of going all the way to the top. I could see myself wheeling and dealing in a large company as a vice president or something. When I graduated from college, I already had a job, so I felt like I was right on track. I still feel on track at the Age-30 Turning Point, but now I have the sense of 'now or never.'

"As for the future, I play out two scenarios in my mind. In one, I keep going for the top, get promoted, and end up in an executive office. I have plenty of money, but maybe I'm not married to Janet anymore. I know I want to have major responsibilities, but it's hard to *picture* myself in charge. It's also hard to picture the life I would be leading—except that I would just be working all the time. The second scenario is more troubling. I picture myself flopping. Not getting promoted. Maybe getting laid off and having to take another job I don't like as well. I picture myself anxious and getting more frightened as I get older and my options diminish. It's actually *that* scenario that drives me. It's a lot clearer to me than the other one. I can imagine how it would feel and what I would be doing. I work like a demon because I can't let that happen."

Feelings now: "Impressed with how powerful that negative image is. And how much I work to keep it from happening."

Janet: "When I went to college, I didn't know what I would study or what I would do after college. I don't even have any real clear memories of high school. I think I felt down or depressed most of that time. I think my parents probably were, too. When I went to college, my only goal was to make good grades.

"I interviewed with my company on campus in the spring of my senior year, and they offered me the job I'm in now. The main thing that happened in my life at this Turning Point was that I met Brian. We're such opposites, but it's like we had known each other for our whole lives. There was never a question but that we would get married.

"At future Turning Points, I see our marriage playing out. We have children; we stay married. The children grow up, and then *they* have children and live close to us, and as we get older we stay together and have close relationships to our children and grandchildren. I don't really see the future too much in terms of my career. If I could quit, I would, so I feel that when Brian is successful enough, I won't be working, but just taking care of the family."

Feelings now: "I found myself irritated by the questions at different Turning Points. I just see the future as being the same, not changing all the time."

Elizabeth

"When I was 18, I did not have a clue about what I would do. I figured I still had plenty of time in college to think about it, and I was having too good a time to worry. I figured, whatever I do, I'll succeed. Actually, the thought that I might *not* succeed never even once occurred to me. The winter of my senior year in college, some companies interviewed on campus, and that's how I got my start. I skyrocketed. It was then that I realized I was just like my dad. In fact, his image is in my mind a lot when I make decisions and go through my day. I feel I have this compass inside my head. I always seem to know exactly what the right move will be. It never fails me. At 29, I was put into the executive pool. One of the youngest. Everything has always seemed right on track—until now, that is. At this Turning Point, nothing seems clear. As I look to the future, I don't think I can keep on this course. I picture wanting more quiet and balance and fulfillment. I don't want my children to grow up without my ever knowing them. I would like to think at age 50 or 60 that I will have a close relationship with my husband."

Feeling now: "I realize that I have been doing everything pretty much as I planned it, but that I'm not very happy with the result. I want my life to be different in the future. But how?"

Carl

"I never planned too much. I just concentrated on taking advantage of the opportunities that presented themselves. I was not a sterling student in either high school or college. My first job after college was in a new business a friend was starting. I ended up running that business for about 18 years. I got married when I was 29—that was the thirties Turning Point. Then I got recruited when I was 40 for the job I just got fired from. The future? I guess I'll just do what I've always done. The questions about retirement and later transitions made me think. I don't have any sense about what retirement looks like. Playing golf? Working? Living in a retirement village? None of it seems to fit me very well."

Feelings now: "Wondering where this is all going."

NEXT CHAPTER: In the next chapter we discuss the basic groundwork of your Personal Vision, your natural talents and abilities. Your natural abilities tell you what kinds of tasks and roles you are naturally suited for, and which you aren't. This is the basic starting information you will need at each of your career Turning Points as you start to construct answers to what you will do with your life.

CHAPTER 4

The Foundation
of Personal Vision:
ABILITIES

FIGURING OUT A PERSONAL VISION MAY BE THE MOST complicated problem any of us ever has solve in life. But the rewards of working through it are immense, whether calculated in terms of success or satisfaction. As we described in Chapter Two, a Personal Vision, to have the most positive impact, must include eight critical factors: stage of development, abilities, skills, interests, personality, values, goals and family of origin. In the last chapter we discussed how your age and life developmental stage influence your Personal Vision. The present chapter deals with the most fundamental aspect of what you bring to your career: your natural talents and abilities.

Before launching into natural abilities, however, we want to explain briefly why a multi-dimensional Personal Vision, as opposed to a single factor or dimension, generates such power in your life.

THE MULTI-DIMENSIONAL PERSONAL VISION

Many writers have thought of *one aspect* of Personal Vision as sufficient to make career decisions. Authors have studied values, goals, abilities, interests, stage of development, skills and personality individually. Each has been proposed as enough information alone to make career decisions or to formulate a career direction. The Lemming Conspiracy, the power of systems to control how you think about your life and career, means that these simple, unitary views are too confining. As powerful individually as each of these factors is, *none* is powerful enough alone to help you escape the power of systems and help you figure out a career direction that makes sense. We created the concept of Personal Vision to integrate all of the factors necessary to give you a complete picture of yourself.

Another, more subtle issue works in many attempts to help people with a life direction. Most experts helping people find career and job direction see their roles in terms of gathering information about people and then telling them what to do. One of the first experts to break with this model was not a counselor or trained expert at all; he was just a businessman trying to solve a problem. He felt that an ideal job should be so specific to the person and to the marketplace that no one could tell you what you should do. You could discover your ideal fit by looking at enough information about yourself. The central insight was that a direction should come from the *inside*, not from the tests or insight of some expert.

The philosophy that informs this book is that you have the answer for your life's work inside yourself. The process we describe is a structure to help you identify it, describe it and put it into action.

Your natural talents underlie any job, role or career you undertake throughout your life. Yet this objective information about what you naturally do easily and what is intrinsically difficult is almost unknown to the vast majority of people as they make critical decisions at career Turning Points.

ABILITIES: WHAT ARE THEY, AND HOW DO YOU KNOW THEM?

Many years ago, an engineer at General Electric was given the task of figuring out what people should do when they applied for work at G.E. Should a prospective employee be a line worker? A supervisor? An engineer? A manager? What training would be most beneficial for a new employee? What kinds of jobs would an employee definitely *not* be suited for? This was before the era of universal college education, and so a person's educational background did not necessarily tell G.E. much about what a person could do.

With no preconceptions about the problem, the engineer started assembling tests that would measure what he called "aptitudes," or natural talents and abilities. He was not interested in what a person could learn through experience. Rather, he wanted to find out the special abilities and talents with which people were born.

A strong aptitude makes it easy for someone to master certain tasks. A weak ability makes it difficult for another person to do the same tasks. We are not talking about intelligence or motivation. Intelligent, highly motivated individuals can accomplish many things for which they have little or no ability. But they may not be happy or satisfied doing it.

The engineer discovered that certain *patterns* of abilities make it easy for a person to work with tools and understand machinery. Other patterns allow people to understand processes and systems, or indicate natural salespeople. Some ability patterns mean that logical, step-by-step explanation of difficult problems is a piece of cake. Still others make managing people in organizations feel like second nature. These patterns remain stable over the many years of a person's working life. A person can't *learn* a pattern of abilities; he or she is either born with it or not.

To the engineer, it became stunningly clear why organizations functioned as inefficiently as they do. In *The Peter Principal*, Laurence Peter forcefully draws a Monty Python-esque picture of organizations in which people who are doing excellent work are promoted rapidly and continuously until they occupy positions for which they are totally incompetent. There they stay until they retire.

Who has not heard a story about a legendary salesman, a killer who would chew through doors to make a sale? His customers like and respect him, and his numbers break all records. As a reward for work well done, management promotes him. He now *manages* 20 salespeople—only to fall flat on his face. Sales plummet; his salespeople hate him and quit; his former customers go elsewhere: a disaster. The Peter Principal? Yes. But of infinitely greater importance, abilities— and the Lemming Conspiracy.

The ability pattern required to make selling to others easy is well known. So is the pattern required to make managing others easy. *But they are completely different patterns.* It is as though we identified a player on a basketball team as a particularly effective rebounder and said, "I've got a great idea, let's make him our ball-handler and play-maker!" Our salesman, so effective at closing a sale with a client, was totally at sea when asked to manage other people who were supposed to close sales. Not because he lacked motivation or intelligence, but because it ran exactly counter to his natural abilities.

There is another current in the story of the salesman. It has to do with systems, and *The Peter Principal* describes accurately what happens. The goal in systems is always to get to the next level. To stay in the same position is to stagnate. To move sideways is to fail. Up or out, that's the rule.

The goal of moving up in systems is external; it is part of the Stress Cycle. Why? Because it has nothing to do with the individual. The salesman would have been much wiser and happier had he remained a killer salesman. But he didn't know that, and his system never brought up the issue. From the perspective of the system, a bright, ambitious young man must move up to get ahead in the organization.

Let us tell you about another man, Joseph, who faced a similar dilemma.

Joseph's Story

Joseph, 41, was a senior partner in a large corporate law firm. He worked most weekends and many nights during the week. For several years he had been managing partner of the law firm. He was generally considered an excellent manager of the firm. He thought of himself as financially comfortable and successful.

Joseph also felt great stress. He did not enjoy his work. It took him away from his young family, but he didn't know what he could do about it. He felt his firm needed him as a manager. He felt his family depended on him to work hard and provide for them. Joseph had enjoyed law for many years after joining his firm, but for the last few years he had not enjoyed his work at all. It felt more like a burden. He worked longer hours now than when he started as a young associate.

Joseph was only vaguely aware of these problems. He probably would not even have described them as problems. From his point of view, what he experienced in his work life was just what everyone experienced. That's just the way things are. His firm was happy with him. His wife accepted the situation as a given and dedicated her time to their children. *No system Joseph was involved with challenged his decisions.*

Joseph went through a corporate program that used the structured approach to creating a Personal Vision we describe in this book. For him, one of the most interesting pieces of objective information he learned was that he has extremely poor natural abilities for management. His natural ability pattern superbly fitted him for law and legal work, but his management duties went completely against his grain. (We should note that natural abilities cannot say whether a person *can* or *cannot* perform a role. Joseph, because he is intelligent and highly motivated, performed the role of manager in his firm extremely well. The problem was that it so far missed his natural ability set, that he was forced to work twice as hard to achieve a result much less satisfying to him personally.)

It would have been easy for Joseph simply to keep doing what he was already doing. His firm benefited from it and expected him to continue. But he was not happy. He quit his role as managing partner—over the protests of the other senior partners. His wife worried over his decision; she was afraid Joseph would have less prestige and pull in the firm.

Joseph's *systems* tried to get him to pay attention to the Stress Cycle. They wanted him to have a short-term focus: he should not make a change because the firm would be upset by changing managing partners. They wanted him to focus on wealth, power and status: what about the prestige of being managing partner? They wanted him to take his direction from the system, not from himself. They wanted his decisions to be reactive, not meaning-driven.

Joseph's systems put this conservative pressure on him not because anyone—his friend and partner, his wife— wanted anything bad for Joseph. They did it because systems resist new information, new rules and new ideas.

Joseph insisted on the change, because he knew objectively he was right. He also set his priorities for his time. He was not going to work on weekends or evenings anymore. He would do this by concentrating on the kind of work he loved, and for which he was particularly well suited.

Joseph's partners were not wild about this at first. But after several months Joseph's team was more productive, and he brought more business into the firm than ever. Besides that, he was happier. His team was happier. And they found another manager.

Astute readers might be asking themselves right now, "Well, how did he manage to go up against all of his systems and make them listen to him? Resigning as managing partner was not something *any* of his systems were prepared to accept."

Joseph's decisions were more complex and involved more issues than abilities. Personality, interests, and family of origin all strongly influenced his actions. We will take up Joseph's story again in Chapter Seven when we talk about the family of origin and its influence.

But just what are abilities? And how do you know what yours are? In the next section, we talk about the most powerful and influential abilities, the Driving Abilities.

THE DRIVING ABILITIES: WHAT THEY ARE AND HOW THEY AFFECT YOUR LIFE

Driving Abilities are so important because they influence, or drive, people whether they are high or low. If you ignore them, you run the significant risk of getting into a role for which your abilities are not well suited. You also run the risk of having a strong Driving Ability that you never use. Our experience has been that a great deal of dissatisfaction at work can be traced to possessing strong abilities, but not using them. We saw this above in Joseph's story. His strong abilities for law were not being used well in his role as a manager. He always felt dissatisfied, unfulfilled.

We will describe four Driving Abilities to give you some idea of what they are and how they relate to each other. The Thought Experiment at the end of the chapter includes a self-report measure to help you assess your Driving Abilities.

CLASSIFICATION

Classification uses your right brain to solve problems. This part of the brain takes information from everywhere—something you heard on the news, something you might have noticed without being aware of it, something somebody said—and pulls it all together at once into a solution. In Classification, your right brain takes a plethora of related and unrelated observations and arrives at a theory to explain them. This is inductive reasoning.

Classification is quick. People who have high Classification love to use it. It's fun. But this quickness and sureness of problem-solving also makes it difficult for people with high Classification to get along easily with people who have other equally valid ways of solving problems.

Let's drop in on the hectic world of Allison, a person with strong Classification ability. We can see how she solves problems, what kinds of tasks are easy for her, and what drives her crazy.

Allison—A Person with Strong Classification. Co-workers describe Allison as quick and self-assured. Given a problem to solve, she knows the answer before anyone even has a chance to explain it to her. She sometimes starts responding to what people say before they can finish their sentences. She has an irritating habit of being right and knowing she is right. She has little patience with people who are slower than she is at seeing the answers. She often feels she is metaphorically tapping her foot, impatiently waiting for her boss to see something that is completely obvious to her.

Allison is happiest when she is fully engaged by problems coming at her thick and furiously, with scarcely time to breathe. She is most miserable when she has nothing new to sink her teeth into.

Allison has high Classification. She doesn't solve problems logically or in a linear fashion; she solves them with her powerful right hemisphere, the one that doesn't speak. Pulling answers for problems together from many different sources simultaneously, people with strong Classification don't necessarily know *how* they get to an answer; they just know what the right answer is. Quickness of problem-solving is one of its defining characteristics.

When you hand a report to a boss, a report that you have worked weeks to make perfect, and he scans it briefly, remarking only that "I would change the order of the chapter titles," he is probably using Classification. People with strong

Classification are quickly able to spot a problem with almost anything—to the general irritation of those around.

Classification demands to be used—more than any other strong ability. A person with high Classification who is stuck in a menial job that requires doing the same thing over and over will be miserable, and perhaps dangerous. One theory holds that many young people who become involved in delinquency as teenagers have high Classification, but low educational and cultural attainment—i.e., no prospects. The most they can hope for is menial labor, which will in no way use their high Classification.

People with high Classification who cannot use this ability at work often *create* problems for themselves, seemingly just to have the opportunity to use it.

To test Classification objectively you must have a problem to solve—not just any problem, but a visual one that involves many separate elements. A problem like this loads almost exclusively on the right hemisphere. People with strong Classification go to the correct solution at once. People with other problem-solving styles must go through a much more laborious process to get to the answer. We cannot, of course, recreate an objective testing session in this book. However, you can figure out an *estimate* of your Classification ability in the Thought Experiment at the end of the chapter.

CONCEPT ORGANIZATION

Concept Organization is the opposite problem-solving style from Classification. Concept Organization uses the left hemisphere to solve problems logically and linearly. Where Classification pulls information from anywhere and everywhere at once, Concept Organization deals with information one step at a time. It lines up parcels of fact and observation in a logical order, so that you can start with a theory and proceed to a logical conclusion—deductive reasoning.

The ability to line up facts logically is generally not as much fun to use as Classification, but it can do things that

Classification cannot. People with high Concept Organization are able to see into the future in a way, because they can start with an idea about what they might want to happen and then logically construct a chain of events that can bring it off.

People with high Concept Organization are also able to communicate easily in words. Words are linear. They are small parcels of information that must be lined up in a logical sequence for communication to happen. You might have had the interesting experience of trying to relate a particularly vivid dream to someone. Dreams are holistic images created in the right hemisphere. They contain complex symbols, images and feelings. As you start to tell someone your dream, you may feel the vividness and richness of the dream disappear as you attempt to put it into words. Words are simply unable to carry the enormously complex images and symbols of dreams. What is left, except occasionally in poetry, is the rather thin and meager content of the dream. But without words, we could not even communicate the content. Without the logical and linear left hemisphere, we could not really communicate complex ideas at all.

Let us look at Jill, who has strong Concept Organization. What kinds of things can she do easily? What kinds of things are difficult? How does she feel about her ability?

Jill—A Person with Strong Concept Organization. Papers, files and folders spill everywhere around Jill's desk and office. A stranger would wonder how she would be able to find anything. But if you were to ask her for a particular piece of paper out of all the piles in her office, she would go to it immediately. It is as if there is a filing system in her head. She knows where everything is according to a logical system that she created, but never thinks about. As a result, she feels no real need for an external system or external order to help her keep track of things.

When Jill's boss told her that they would need to prepare an annual report, she replied that it would take two weeks. She had immediately assessed everything else she was working on, re-prioritized all of it, figured out the tasks she would need to accomplish, and allowed some extra time for unknowns. All of this was completely obvious to her, but she had worked with her boss long enough to know that he didn't think like she did. He had worked with her long enough to know that if she said two weeks, this was probably the best estimate he could get, even if he didn't immediately see why.

Jill is able to organize the thousand details of her life and family without strain or noticeable effort. Sometimes, occasionally, things happen too fast at the office, or there are too many projects competing for her attention. At these times, she shows some strain and anxiety. She can't figure out what she ought to do *first* or, even worse for her, what she ought just to leave undone.

Jill can write more clearly and logically than her boss. But she likes it better when he gives her the direction he wants her to take in a letter. She knows that he sometimes has an idea that seems like it's from outer space to her, but that ends up being effective anyway. Jill doesn't like doing anything by the seat of her pants. When someone asks her what her gut reaction is to something, she will reply with a logical conclusion. She knows she works most effectively when she's given time to figure out conclusions logically. She knows she is least effective when she is overwhelmed by multiple tasks that need to be done at once.

Jill's ability to solve problems logically feels almost invisible to her. She is often not aware of using it; nor is she often aware of how powerful it is for her. She assumes that everyone probably thinks the same way she does.

Objective measures of Concept Organization give participants a logical, linear, verbal task to perform. The left brain can do this task quickly and with ease, but it is almost impossible for the right brain to tackle it. You can get a sense of your Concept Organization ability with the self-report quiz in the Thought Experiment.

TWO FREQUENT ABILITY PATTERNS

Steve—A Consultant's Pattern of Abilities. Steve is a corporate consultant who sees executives all day long in one-to-one mentoring relationships. He must constantly think on his feet. His clients ask him about business concerns, personal problems, tricky staff questions, tactical issues, and long-term strategies. He never really knows what a session will be like beforehand. Steve is good at this, and he likes it. He has both high Classification and high Concept Organization.

When a client asks him about a problem, Steve usually knows how to tackle it before he or she finishes talking. He describes it as having a picture of the answer. This is his strong Classification ability. But when Steve responds, it is not in a picture or any kind of impressionistic way. Rather, he gives a closely reasoned, carefully thought-out summary of his point of view with his thoughts and arguments compellingly marshaled. When Steve solves the problem—when he gets a picture of the solution—he uses Classification. When he presents his point of view, he uses Concept Organization.

Steve works by using both Classification and Concept Organization. This is most efficient and productive for him. He could do his job with many other patterns of abilities, but he would have to go about his job differently to be equally satisfied and productive.

John—An Executive's Pattern of Abilities. One of Steve's clients is John. He is older than Steve, and has been an executive in his company for many years. He started as a young trainee right out of college and worked his way up through the layers of the organization. He says of himself that he has made every mistake in the book—some more than once. But he developed an instinct over the years that now makes it easy for him to provide a clear and accurate direction for the people he manages.

When someone asks John his gut feeling about something, he responds immediately with his gut feeling. He has an unerring sense of what people should be in what jobs, and he has a sure ability to provide the kind of work environment in which people can do their most productive work. John is an experiential problem-solver—he scores low on both Classification and Concept Organization.

There has been a great deal of interest among psychologists about these experiential problem-solvers. They arrive at an answer to a problem by checking with their *experience* of similar problems in the past. What psychologists have found, often to their surprise, is that this is often a much more direct and efficient route to a solution than trying to solve it through logic like someone with high Concept Organization or by coming up with a new solution to every problem, like a person with high Classification.

People with high Classification and/or high Concept Organization are often one step removed from their experiences. They often feel and act as though their thoughts and conclusions were more real than actual reality. People who are low in both of these abilities are able to access their *experiences* more easily than others.

Steve was often struck by John's ability to say, "*This* is what is important here. I won't worry if we never get to *that*." But when John started with the company as a young man, he was sometimes overawed by others his age who seemed quicker or more able to handle complex projects. He tried a lot of different roles, failed a lot when he first started, but rose steadily because he was able to manage people so effectively. To him, this talent was like breathing. "What's the big deal?" But his ability to lead a team, give it a goal and vision, and create the conditions for each person in which he or she could function most effectively made him able to rise much higher than many of the bright stars he started with.

John had discovered how he worked best, and it was different from how others work. John's pattern of abilities made it supremely easy for him to manage, motivate, and direct the work of other people. An important part of that pattern was that John was such a strong experiential problem-solver. This pattern made it slower, perhaps, for John in the beginning— experiential problem-solving requires experience—but he eventually discovered that by working through others, he could make his best and highest contribution. And be a lot happier.

IDEA PRODUCTIVITY

When high, Idea Productivity is second only to Classification in its impact on a person's life. Idea Productivity describes the rate of flow of ideas. A person with high Idea Productivity, if asked to think of solutions to a problem, might come up with 25 different ones in the space of five minutes. A person with low Idea Productivity might come up with two in the same period of time. Idea Productivity refers to *quantity*, not quality or creativity. It might be that both of the ideas of the person with low Idea Productivity would end up being useful, while only one of the high Idea Productivity person's many ideas ever help. High Idea Productivity *alone* does not predict how creative a person's ideas are. People with high Idea Productivity find that ideas and thoughts come to them constantly, even when they wish they wouldn't.

Andrew—A Person with Strong Idea Productivity. Andrew loves selling. He can sell anything to anyone. He loves finding just the right "hook" to get someone interested. He loves hearing their objections so that he can deftly steer them around the obstacle. He never knows what he is going to say; he always flies by the seat of his pants when he is making a sale. He picks up on nuances of meaning and speech and uses them to help his customer hear his pitch. He is overjoyed when a potential customer has a new objection because it gives him a challenge. The challenge is to develop, instantaneously, exactly the message that *this* potential customer will be able to hear. Andrew is a master at this.

What he does not do well is keep records. It's too much detail. He might get started on lists for his customers, only to drop it and start on something else in less than 60 seconds. A few minutes later, he will drop that, too. Andrew has a hard time paying attention to details for long periods at a time, but not because he is distracted by outside noises. He is distracted from the inside, by his own thoughts. As soon as he starts working on something, a completely unrelated thought strikes him and takes his attention. No sooner does he start thinking about that, than another thought interrupts.

Andrew's friends sometimes get irritated because he is always interrupting them. Andrew's boss has noticed that he is a wonderful salesperson, but has his limits when asked to think about strategy. Andrew will generate 10 alternatives, none of which seem particularly creative or useful. But Andrew can persuade anyone to come around to his point of view. That's what makes him such a powerful and effective salesperson.

Idea Productivity is such a powerful ability because it demands to be used almost constantly. A person with high Idea Productivity who is asked to concentrate on the same task all day long will be miserable and unproductive. A person like this may wonder why his or her concentration is so bad, but actually it is just a poor use of his or her abilities.

To measure Idea Productivity objectively, you simply count the number of ideas that occur to a person when given a standard problem to solve in a given span of time. You can get a sense of your Idea Productivity from the Thought Experiment questions at the end of the chapter.

SPATIAL RELATIONS

Spatial Relations ability is the best understood and most researched of all of the abilities. It is the ability to manipulate and envision three-dimensional objects and three-dimensional space in your mind. When we measure Spatial Relations, we give participants a task in which they are required to "see" a three-dimensional object in space and then mentally rotate it to "see" how it would look from the other side.

In all studies in the literature, men score higher on Spatial Relations as a group than women do. This is deceptive, however, because many individual women score extremely high on Spatial Relations, and many individual men score low. Without actually measuring it, you can't tell exactly how high or low on Spatial Relations any one person is.

In general, high school courses and most college courses do not use Spatial Relations ability. Many people score high in Spatial Relations on objective measures who had absolutely no knowledge or sense of this ability. It had been invisible to them because they had never had an opportunity to use it.

People who are high in Spatial Relations have a particular affinity and feel for *things*. They like to work with tools. They enjoy making things. They are interested in how things work. They like to figure out how things are constructed. They are interested in the structure of things. They often are engineers, physicians and scientists. For a person with high Spatial Relations ability, abstract concepts never seem real. A table feels real. But dealing with abstractions like feelings and relationships, like a counselor might do all day long, would eventually feel empty to a person high in this ability.

Some experts feel that if you are strong in Spatial Relations ability, you need to use it in your work. If you don't, you run the risk of never feeling fully engaged with what you do all day long.

Elaine—A Person with Strong Spatial Relations Ability. Elaine is a successful architect. She went all the way through high school and most of the way through college taking liberal arts courses, never realizing that she had strong Spatial Relations abilities. She could never identify what she wanted to do in life, and when she was a junior in college, she decided to take a year off. She spent this year teaching skiing in Aspen. During this year off, she met an architect, and talked to him at length about what he did and how he got to do what he did.

Elaine was fascinated. She began reading books and inquiring about architecture schools. She found a program that would admit her, but she had to spend an extra year in college. She then got a master's degree in architecture.

Elaine is now designing and building several visitors' centers for Native American tribal councils. This job challenges her to help people of European, African, or Asian cultural backgrounds understand something of an alien Native American culture through the architecture of the centers. This task requires all of her abilities and background. She must envision the structure and the space that people will occupy. She must be able to see it from the point of view of someone looking at the building from the outside *and* from the point of view of someone inside, looking at the exhibits.

It is interesting that even Elaine's background in liberal arts has been helpful to her. She has had to spend a great deal of time with Native American tribal councils listening and learning what is important to them and figuring out how to extract that and interpret it to people with cultural backgrounds that have no real point of reference to Native American cultures.

As Elaine moves from the design to the actual building of the projects, she will be more engaged with the materials and structure of the buildings themselves. She is able to envision how each of the materials contributes to the overall look, stability and strength of the projects. She also deals with the scheduling and timing of the projects and how to get the buildings to come together in a rational, orderly way.

Spatial Relations ability makes it possible for Elaine to do all of these tasks easily and well. In fact, the only difficult part for her is communicating her vision of the space and structures to people who do not see mentally in three dimensions as easily as she does.

A fit in one's career as precise and creative as Elaine's is very seldom really an accident; nor is it simple. It weaves together many strands of the person's life into a whole fabric.

Natural abilities are the place to begin Personal Visions, but they are never *enough* to make accurate and creative decisions about your career. All eight factors are vitally important, and weaving them together may require an epic creative leap. This is why it is so important to follow a structure when creating your Personal Vision. You can be sure this way that you are getting to all the pieces.

THOUGHT EXPERIMENT C:
Driving Abilities

NOTE TO READERS
If you wish to make full use of the Thought Experiments in this book, we urge you to take advantage of the Special Offer described on page 240. This offer gives you, as a purchaser of this book, a special discounted rate for taking the Highlands Ability Battery at a Highlands Program office near you. The self-report measures included here can give you some indicators of your Driving Abilities, but the objective, carefully validated measures of the Highlands Ability Battery can give you much more information, more objectively. In addition, you can find out about many other, more specialized abilities, have a two-hour individual conference with one of our counselors, and receive a detailed written report on your results. If you are contemplating any significant career decisions, this can be highly valuable information, and will give you a completely objective foundation upon which to build your Personal Vision.

SELF-REPORT MEASURES OF DRIVING ABILITIES

You can get an idea of your Driving Abilities by answering the following questions about yourself.

In your Personal Vision Notebook, using the scale below, write down the number of how well or poorly each of the following statements describes you:

THE HIGHLANDS PROGRAM
DRIVING ABILITY QUIZ
Use this scale to rate your response to each item:

Not at all like me		Mostly not like me		Sometimes yes, sometimes no			Some-what like me		Exactly describes me
1	2	3	4	5	6	7	8	9	10

1. I *like* problem-solving and arrive at solutions very quickly.
2. I sometimes feel restless waiting for others to 'get it.'
3. I usually know exactly how to solve a problem.
4. Mostly I know what someone will say before they finish talking.
5. My solutions are usually the best ones.
6. I can organize and explain information easily.
7. I can plan quickly and well.
8. I appreciate a logical order to things.
9. It's easy for me to see the logical steps for future plans. I can easily see how to get there from here.
10. I feel more comfortable thinking through things step by step than just leaping into a solution.
11. When trying to solve a problem, I know I'll think of many ideas.
12. I am good in brainstorming sessions.
13. Ideas come so quickly to me that sometimes I interrupt others who are talking.
14. Ideas frequently crowd my mind.
15. Sometimes I am distracted by my own thoughts.
16. I am often interested in how machines work.
17. I have an intuitive understanding of machines and structures.
18. I like to work with tools.
19. I enjoy working with things I can touch and see.
20. I like to have a real product or 'thing' to see and touch when I finish something.

Add up your scores as follows:

Questions 1-5 _____ Classification

Total score, questions 1-5:		
	Low	5-30
	Medium	31-40
	High	41-50

Questions 6-10 _____ Concept Organization

Total score, 6-10:		
	Low	5-30
	Medium	31-40
	High	41-50

Questions 11-15 _____ Idea Productivity

Total score, 11-15:		
	Low	5-30
	Medium	31-40
	High	41-50

Questions 16-20 _____ Spatial Relations

Total score, 16-20:		
	Low	5-30
	Medium	31-40
	High	41-50

You should be aware that this self-report quiz cannot provide the same kind of validated, precise and accurate measurement of abilities as objectively administered work samples.

HIGH CLASSIFICATION

If your self-report score is in the high range, this can mean that Classification is a powerful ability for you, and may influence almost every aspect of your working life.

This is an ability that demands to be used if you have it as strongly as your self-report score indicates. Almost anyone who has this ability strongly gets positive enjoyment from using it. The flip side of that statement is important to remember, however. If you find yourself in a position that does not use this ability, you may be unhappy with your work.

The high Classification person loves to solve problems and to figure things out. This person enjoys change and challenge. There is nothing he or she likes better than taking on a new task, because learning something new uses this ability.

MEDIUM CLASSIFICATION

Your self-report score is in the mid-range in this ability. Classification is a rather powerful ability and your score in the mid-range indicates that you should take it into account when thinking about your work role. In a sense, you have more of a choice about using your Classification ability than if it were either high or low. You should be able to work in fast-paced environments or more stable, less chaotic environments. It may be that you will choose one type of work environment over another for reasons unrelated to Classification. Being in the mid-range on this ability gives you that option.

LOW CLASSIFICATION

Your self-report score indicates that you may find any work situation stressful that is chronically chaotic and that requires rapid-fire problem-solving with very little information. You will be happier and more productive in a work environment that is more stable and more structured.

The strength of your score in Classification is that you have the ability to persevere long enough to become proficient. You can become expert by acquiring increasing levels of knowledge and experience.

HIGH CONCEPT ORGANIZATION

Your high score in Concept Organization suggests an aptitude for any planning activity. In being able to see the logical sequences of events, you can predict, order and plan schedules for when things are going to happen. Even more important, this is the primary ability needed to communicate ideas to other people. Since you may be able to arrange ideas easily into a logical sequence, creating written materials and presentations of ideas that make sense to others may be easy for you. You may be able to see how all of the pieces of a project fit together to make a coherent whole. You will be able to use this ability effectively in any work in which there is a recurring need to organize materials or information.

People who are high in Concept Organization find that they want to use this ability often. Most people have ample opportunity to use it in their everyday lives, both at home and at work, and so we don't see people who are tremendously unhappy because it is not a part of their jobs.

MEDIUM CONCEPT ORGANIZATION

In the workplace, Concept Organization is a fundamental ability. Your self-report score indicates that you should be able to perform essential work and office tasks—planning, predicting, scheduling and communicating—with relative ease.

LOW CONCEPT ORGANIZATION

Your self-report score on Concept Organization can be an advantage in an environment that places a premium on action. If a person must act quickly and decisively, the kind of logical planning that is the hallmark of Concept Organization is actually counter-productive. It delays action.

Your score in Concept Organization means that it is relatively laborious for you to plan, organize, and prioritize internally. It is much easier for you to use various external means of organization. These could include schedules, lists of priorities, or lists of tasks to accomplish. People who are in the low range in Concept Organization frequently like to have their external world fairly neat and orderly. This helps them stay focused on what they feel is important.

HIGH IDEA PRODUCTIVITY

Your self-report score on Idea Productivity indicates that you may have many ideas flowing through your thoughts during any given period of time. It is important to remember that Idea Productivity is not an ability that you can turn off at will. These ideas occur to you whether you want them to or not. Whenever possible, you will be much happier and more productive when you can use your Idea Productivity in rapid idea production, problem solving, and adjusting to new ideas, rather than trying to struggle against it.

Conversely, you will feel very confined by a task that requires long attention to meticulous detail, or highly detailed follow-through on someone else's plans and ideas. You are possibly capable of such concentration, but you will be constantly struggling against your Idea Productivity to achieve it. You will feel much more involved and fulfilled in your work if you have a real outlet for your flow of ideas during most of your working day.

MEDIUM IDEA PRODUCTIVITY

Your score in the medium range in Idea Productivity indicates that you will have some of the advantages of a high score, as well as some advantages of a low score. You are able to come up with ideas at a sufficient rate to be useful to you in solving problems and overcoming objections. You will enjoy being able to use this skill at times. Your rate of idea production is such that you probably feel somewhat confined by a task that requires long attention to meticulous detail, or highly detailed follow-through on someone else's plans and ideas. You are capable of such concentration, but you will not enjoy it as a complete description of your work day. You will feel much more involved and fulfilled in your work if you have some outlet for your flow of ideas during some portion of your working day.

Some uses for your rate or flow of new ideas can be in dreaming up solutions for problems, or in "selling" your point of view to others. You are in an ideal position to have enough concentration to work out a solution to a problem and dream up alternatives, and then adroitly overcome others' objections.

LOW IDEA PRODUCTIVITY

Idea Productivity confers an advantage whether you are high or low, provided you choose the appropriate work environment. Your self-report score in the low range in Idea Productivity may indicate that you are able to focus well, and work without undue distraction on a given project for a considerable length of time. You will probably work most effectively in a stable rather than a volatile work situation, where your ability to maintain focus undistracted is a positive strength. You will probably want to avoid being in situations in which you persuade or sell to others in an impromptu manner.

In work areas requiring a high degree of concentration, a low score in Idea Productivity is a distinct advantage. Your score in Idea Productivity will be helpful to you in any task that requires you to pay attention to details and follow through to a conclusion on ideas and plans.

HIGH SPATIAL RELATIONS

This is an extremely valuable ability in many areas of business. It is, of course, a fundamental ability for someone interested in design, construction, manufacture and technology. This ability allows a person to experiment mentally with different options or arrangements of elements or objects without actually having to see them.

An important consideration to keep in mind, however, is that eventually someone who is high in Spatial Relations will want to see the physical result of what he or she is doing. People who score high in this ability need to have their hands on something or produce something. They are most at home with provable facts, products, machinery and tools. Many roles at work do not deal in such tangibles. Roles and tasks that deal mainly in ideas, relationships, information or influence can end up feeling quite unreal to a person high in Spatial Relations. Some experts in the field of abilities consider this one of the most important factors to take into account when planning a work role.

There is a compelling quality to Spatial Relations/

Visualization in the sense that people who are high in it eventually feel pulled to use it. Often this pull does not make itself felt until a person is middle-aged. It is most often experienced as a wish to do something real—to have a tangible result of one's efforts at the end of the day.

MEDIUM SPATIAL RELATIONS

A score in the mid-range on this ability is sometimes difficult to interpret. Typically, people either have this ability or they don't. People who are high in Spatial Relations usually want to see the results of their actions in a concrete and immediate way. If they manage a business, they are more satisfied if the business produces a concrete product such as a chair, rather than an abstract product such as information. Your score in the mid-range on this ability indicates that you may have the ability to visualize the concrete results of what you are doing in your work. If so, you may want to consider being sure to use this ability on a daily basis.

LOW SPATIAL RELATIONS

A self-report score on this measure in the low, or abstract, range has several important implications. People in the abstract range are typically quite comfortable in work that deals with people, relationships, information or influence. They do not usually experience a strong wish to be involved in the concrete world of physical objects in their work. Training, managing, counseling, law and accounting are all examples of typically abstract work roles.

FOUR STORIES: ABILITIES

Tracy

"I have all of the Driving Abilities very strongly. It means I can do anything, basically. It's called a multi-ability pattern. The good side of it is that I have a lot of strong abilities. The bad side of it is that it makes it hard for me to choose anything that will use all of those abilities. At least I don't feel so crazy that it's been hard for me to figure out a direction.

"Finding out about my abilities was interesting, because I never thought of myself as a scientist or anything. But I could do science or medicine. It might be that law or even psychology would not use all of my abilities. I guess I don't really know that much more than when I started, but at least I know I can do something else. I realize now why I hate my job so much. It doesn't use any of my abilities. I guess I had lost a lot of confidence. After I graduated, I suddenly realized, 'I don't have a clue here.'"

Feeling at this point: "Better. More hopeful."

Brian and Janet

Brian: "Well, my abilities were right on target. High Classification, High Idea Productivity. It's no wonder I thrive on the pace at work. I feel like I have ideas and energy running out my fingertips. Whatever I do, I need to be in a work setting like the one I'm in. It seems perfect for me."

Feeling at this point: "I feel good about my job. Maybe why I feel so stressed is other things besides the job itself."

Janet: "The main thing I found out was that I like to take my time and solve problems logically. I have very high Concept Organization. I get frustrated with customers because they are so unreasonable. I can show them exactly why something happened, but it doesn't make any difference to them. It drives me crazy. I think my ability pattern is a hindrance rather than a help in my job."

Feelings at this point: "Interested. More confident."

Elizabeth

"I'm at the mid-point in both Classification and Concept Organization. My Idea Productivity and Spatial Relations are both low. I like to have problems to sink my teeth into. But not too many at the same time. I can see why I like my job—when it's not totally overwhelming. I can also see why it's so easy for me to deal with problems."

Feelings now: "This means a lot to me. I know how to position myself better at work. I feel encouraged."

Carl

"I have low scores on all the Driving Abilities. This means I am an experiential problem-solver. I don't stop and figure out a logical solution. I usually solve problems at work by thinking of some situation I was in before that this reminds me of. Then I have a good idea about what to do. I know I have a strong innate understanding of what makes people tick. If you put me in a group of people, they always seem to elect me the leader. People listen to me. At least they have ever since I turned thirty-five or so."

Feelings now: "Still hopeful. Still wondering where all of this is going. Getting a little impatient to find an answer."

NEXT CHAPTER: In the next chapter we continue the construction of your Personal Vision. Abilities form the groundwork, but to become a useful tool the structure of a Personal Vision must include your skills, interests and personality.

CHAPTER 5

The Building Blocks of Personal Vision:

SKILLS, INTERESTS *and* PERSONALITY

A PERSONAL VISION MUST HAVE A DEFINITE STRUC-
ture and coherence. It should embrace and comprehend your
whole life, not just the hours you spend making a living. It's
often easy to "forget" part of your life—just leave it out of
your plans. If you leave a piece out, you run the risk of being
subtly trapped by your systems into the Lemming Conspiracy.
As we saw in the last chapter, your natural, inborn talents and
gifts form the base, or foundation, of your Personal Vision. In
this chapter, we will look at the body and substance of the
structure: your skills and experience, your interests and fascinations, and your personality—how you habitually interact
with others.

SKILLS AND EXPERIENCE: WHAT HAVE YOU LEARNED IN LIFE?

When Dan was 42, he had a sudden insight: He hated his job,
and he would rather do anything than go to work that day.
Everyone may have this feeling from time to time, but for him,

the feeling didn't go away. In fact, it got worse. Eventually, he was sure that the only way to save his sanity was to quit his job altogether, move to the beach, and, using his retirement money, open a shop for tourists. He went so far as to check real-estate listings at his favorite beach resort and to call his pension manager to find out how much money he could with-draw when he quit.

Fortunately, Dan didn't do that. He had been a corporate lawyer for 16 years, had never sold anything to the public, had never run an entrepreneurial business, and didn't really know the first thing about retail trade. It was a fantasy of a more relaxed, easier life, without the stress and greed that he encountered every day in his clients and in their adversaries.

Dan faced a number of problems with this dream of a beach-front surf shop. But the main one was that it didn't take into account the enormous wealth of education and experience that he had so carefully built over the 42 years of his life.

Most people are not aware of the richness of their own skills. Many simply overlook their most powerful and effective skills because they have always used them so effectively. Their most significant skills don't seem like important assets, because they're easy. When asked to name their best skills, most people will name something that was particularly diffi-cult for them to learn. Dan would have said, for instance, that the only thing he had learned in 16 years of lawyering was how to plug most loopholes in most contracts.

In a seminar, Dan told a story about some events from his childhood that meant something to him. He had nearly flunked math in the eighth grade, but by dint of labor and will, had managed to press on in math through high school with mostly B's and C's—the first time he had been unable to earn virtually effortless A's. He felt tremendously frustrated at first, believing that school was really the only thing he could do, and now *that* wasn't going well. Eventually he decided that maybe he should try something besides school. And he did. He learned to play the guitar, started a rock band, crafted music and lyrics, wrote humorous pieces for a school magazine and ended as editor-in-chief of the school newspaper his senior year.

Dan didn't see what was special about this story. It was just what he had done in high school. It remained mildly embarrassing to him that math was almost totally beyond his ability to understand. But other people, people outside Dan's systems, saw much more in this story than laboring through a difficult school subject. You, the reader, can undoubtedly see much more, too. It was just invisible to Dan.

Dan's story is actually quite rich. The other participants in the seminar turned up dozens of skills and talents Dan had clearly shown in an event he thought of as a failure. For starters, he had transformed this frustration in high school into a positive, meaningful event in his life. By accepting a limit, he had been able to branch out into other, nonacademic pursuits. He loved music and enjoyed playing in a band with others. His real talent was writing, though. He wrote most of the bands' songs. He wrote for the newspaper, and made people laugh at themselves with wry columns. Later, as editor-in-chief, he was able to get other writers to meet deadlines and to organize all of the hundreds of pieces that went into a finished newspaper. He assumed the responsibility of directing stories and editing writers' copy easily. He could tell writers that they had to cut their stories in half, or that a story didn't have enough back-up information, in a way they could accept. He got them to work within limits, instead of fighting them.

As the seminar participants told Dan what *they* recognized in his story, it occurred to him that he helped his clients see alternatives where they saw none, and he helped them accept realistic limits where they were not wanting any at all.

Dan had never ascribed any importance to the fact that he had formed and led a band of high school boys. Nor had he thought much about his role as editor of the school newspaper. What both of these roles had in common was holding people with strong personalities and strong agendas together and steering them toward a common goal—a goal he had first articulated and set out to accomplish. This, of course, was exactly what he so deftly managed when he negotiated agreements between clients. Realizing this gave Dan an entirely new perspective on his skills. His skills made him a great corporate lawyer; but he could also use them in many other fields. As he started to engage his experience and skills, attempting to figure out how to use instead of discard them, the fantasy of a beach-front shell shop made less and less sense.

Dan realized that the beach shop was an expression of a goal: a less hectic and stressful life. He knew he would be throwing away some of his most important assets if he were to throw over corporate deal-making altogether. He pondered how he could reach his goal but also stay with his firm and a job that fit him so well. By working with his partners, setting clear limits, and sticking to them, he was able to cut back his stress seriously. He now spends more time at the beach. He recently published a story in a literary monthly.

You can see that a crucial part of Dan's story, once he figured out how important his skills were, became naming and ordering his life goals. In Chapter Six, we talk more about articulating and prioritizing goals.

In the Thought Experiment at the end of this chapter, you will find a variation of the exercise Dan used to discover his real skills. It will help you understand your skills and experiences and how they contribute to what you do well. Remember, Dan's real skills were invisible to him until he did a specific exercise. This is true of virtually everyone. We designed the exercise in the Thought Experiment to help you *see* the most important things you have learned in your lifetime.

In the next section, you'll learn about one of the most overlooked factors of all: interests. Yet interests sometimes define the most direct path to creativity and enthusiasm.

INTERESTS: DIRECT LINE TO WHERE YOU REALLY LIVE

"Follow your bliss." Joseph Campbell's oft-quoted line could not offer a better or truer piece of advice. When we talk to people who have led particularly full and satisfying lives and ask them how they managed to find just the career that suited them best, they all say some version of the same thing: "I followed my nose." What appears to be extraordinary luck or the product of unusual confluence of talents is actually neither.

When you pay attention to what is personally interesting and fascinating to you, you get to include this magical pull in your career. You can be more creative and much happier. Work doesn't have to seem like work. The fact that somebody pays you to do it can seem like the most extraordinary luck of all.

For most people, "interests" and "work" are like two separate boxes. There is rarely any connection between them. By taking a careful look at what you are drawn to, and fascinated by, you can discover your real source of creativity and energy.

When people assign their passions to a box labeled "not work" and relegate it to those times when they are not utterly exhausted by the routine of their days, it often takes some focused attention to bring interests to the forefront and make them important. Some successful executives in the middle of a workshop look up suddenly in surprise and say, "I never realized that my interests could have anything to do with work."

Richard's Story, continued

You may remember the story of Richard, in Chapter Three, the 41-year-old veteran insurance executive who had thought his only alternative was to quit. It turned out that his interests became a key to discovering satisfaction in his job. He had many passions in life but felt he could never get to them if he kept working as he had been. We have seen how finding out about his Classification ability made some of his discontent make sense to him. But what should he *do*?

Richard completed a long-term exercise on interests very

much like the one you will find in the Thought Experiment at the end of this chapter. He realized that the hundreds of ideas, images and people that came his way every day fascinated him. From long habit, as soon as some idea grabbed his attention, he just as quickly let it go. He couldn't deal with it. He had no energy. He had a responsible job, a family, a life. He had no time to pursue anything like that. He became just a little more resigned inside.

Richard "caught" the many images, thoughts, ideas, words, stories, pictures, articles, people and events that momentarily grabbed his interest. He cut them out, wrote them down, and made brief notes about them. He became adept at holding onto a spark of interest long enough to identify it and make a record of it. He saved all of his records.

After a few weeks, he sorted the records into groups. Almost all of his interests lumped together into three broad categories: music and dance, art and photography, and one that he labeled loosely "adventure." These categories had remained stable for years. He had *always* been interested in them.

It dawned on Richard that his interests and fascinations, so long ignored and pushed down in the name of adulthood, could give his life more texture and substance. He began to take them more seriously. He came to want to build a life in which they could play a role.

Once that goal was clear, things changed rapidly. As so often happens, when Richard knew what he wanted clearly enough, a way opened for him to obtain it. Actually, a way had always been there; he had just never noticed it until he realized he needed it.

Richard's insurance company had instituted a policy of flex time for employees several years previously. He had been aware of this policy, but as an executive he had understood that the policy had nothing to do with him. It was for tellers and bookkeepers, mostly women who had to deal with child care.

As Richard ruminated on the question of how to pursue his passions in life, a memo came across his desk about flex time. He put in a request to his boss to work four days and take Wednesdays off. He would work the same number of hours, but not Wednesdays. He would then be able to pursue other ideas and interests outside of work.

The reaction was volcanic. His boss explained carefully, as if to someone slightly dim, that the policy was not for employees like Richard. Richard knew he could win, though, because, as it happened, his boss had written the policy. It had been a political move to make the company seem more forward-thinking. Of the company's 20,000 employees, fewer than 30 had put in requests.

This is an example of the Lemming Conspiracy at work. The insurance company had a limited number of answers, and actively resisted any new ones. No one behaved malevolently. But a system does not care what Richard wants from his life. Had Richard quit his job, his boss and friends would have been surprised, and his co-workers would have been momentarily disturbed. But there would be a new person in his spot soon, and the system would proceed, having learned nothing.

Before his quest, Richard's boss, friends, and co-workers, and Richard himself, for that matter, defined Richard's options as the options of the system. It was only when Richard got *outside* the system and went through the structured process for gaining a Personal Vision that he was able to see himself more clearly and see that many more options existed than those the system offered.

Richard did win. He now takes Wednesday off, and has for two years. He plans to pick out something each year from one of his major groupings of interests to pursue and explore. This year music takes center stage. He is learning to play the violin and he and his wife are learning to dance. He doesn't know where this will lead, and he doesn't care. It adds joy to his life; he feels more productive at work.

Richard feels his life is completely different now than it was two years ago. His heightened sense of creativity is a perfectly normal byproduct of actively pursuing his fascinations. He is just as productive, but a lot happier. The insurance company benefited because it kept one of its most valuable employees. Richard benefited because he feels he is *living* his life for the first time in years.

But there is more to Richard's story. In defining his Personal Vision, that is, getting a complete picture of what he wanted his life to look like over time, Richard became very clear about the kinds of jobs he liked to do at work and also the kinds of projects that made best use of his particular set of talents and abilities. Now, if a project comes his way for which he knows he is not suited and would not enjoy, he turns it down. On the other hand, when someone proposes a project that Richard knows will be perfect for him, he jumps at once. Co-workers often express surprise at Richard's certainty. Sometimes he is more enthusiastic about a project than the person who tentatively proposed it in the first place. He has become something of a guru among his contemporaries in the company. Often, someone will pull him aside in whispered tones and ask him how he did it. The most difficult part of explaining his story is trying to convince people that the key is not in how he put it to his boss or in the structure of his proposal, but rather in learning about himself.

When we learn about our interior selves to create a Personal Vision, it is important to understand how we relate to others. This is the next building block of Personal Vision, personality.

PERSONALITY: THE INTERPERSONAL ENVIRONMENT

Many people have become excited and enthusiastic about personality, only to draw a blank when faced with using this information in a day-to-day setting. A popular personality inventory workshop becomes the talk of the office for a few days. But a month later everyone has forgotten about it, and not much has really changed. Experiences such as these may lead to cynicism about the usefulness of personality measures; however, in the context of the whole person, personality is an important piece of the puzzle.

One of the most limiting aspects of personality, as it has been used in business and corporate settings, is that it is so often used in isolation. Zealots proclaim, "Hi, I'm an ENTJ," or "Hi, I'm a Proactive-Idealist," as though this were sufficient introduction. Some feel that this kind of shorthand explains all there is to know about themselves. Nothing could be further from the truth. This is an example of using one of the building blocks of Personal Vision to stand for the whole structure. But it's not enough.

Personality testing carries at least two other burdens. First, almost all traditional personality testing is self-reported. You tell the test about yourself, and then the results of the test tell you what you just said. Obviously, no one knows you as well as you do yourself. On the other hand, you can't very well have an objective view of yourself, either. Furthermore, consultants and others have often used personality testing to predict patterns of behavior and predict how well a person will perform on a given job. Research suggests this is a misuse of personality testing. Personality patterns tend to change over time. In fact, any given personality pattern shown on a test should probably be taken as more or less true only within a two-year window around the testing itself. As for trying to predict overall job performance by personality testing (or worse, by interest testing), this is a clear abuse. Many more factors than personality affect job performance. Unless *all* of these factors are taken into account, any prediction is subject to serious error.

This said, when personality testing is used by individuals as one aspect of judgment about their own lives and careers, it can be powerful and informative.

The idea that certain patterns describe how we habitually interact with our fellow humans is an extremely old one. From the Greeks on, philosophers and pundits have described types of people engaging in more or less consistent patterns of interacting.

Some people love to talk to others; some prefer to be by themselves. But even the most garrulous extrovert likes to be alone sometimes. And even the most intense introvert gets lonely eventually. We are not really talking about something that can be measured with 100 percent accuracy. Personality traits are usually described by two ends of a continuum. Extroversion, for instance, is at one end of the continuum, introversion at the other. People are located somewhere between the two.

We will describe two personality dimensions we have found to be particularly helpful in thinking about what you might want to do with your life: extroversion *vs.* introversion and generalist *vs.* specialist. In the Thought Experiment we included a brief self-report quiz you can use to form an estimate of where you are on each of these dimensions, and a short summary of how your score describes your pattern of interacting.

INTROVERSION-EXTROVERSION

You can think of Introversion and Extroversion in terms of energy. Where do you get your energy? When an extrovert is tired after a busy day and wants to recharge, he or she wants to talk to someone. The extrovert gets energy back from the interaction. For very strong extroverts, nothing seems very real unless they have discussed it with someone. Often strong extroverts think through their ideas as they talk them over with a friend. Talking about an idea is an important part of the whole process of thinking for the extrovert. Extroverts like being around other people, being in groups and being in the know. At parties, extroverts get around and see everyone.

Not so the introvert. For the introvert who is tired after a day at the office, nothing is so restful and recharging as coming home, going through the mail, petting the dog, reading the paper, and not talking to anyone. No matter how skillful and comfortable in interacting with others the introvert learns to be, it is always work. There is always energy going out. Introverts like to think ideas through before they share them. When they share ideas, especially personal ones, introverts feel best when they have a long history of trust with the other person. Introverts don't enjoy groups. When at parties, they often have a good time by finding an old friend and spending the evening talking to that one person.

No personality dimension is absolute. However, we have found that understanding the direction of your own tendency can be important when figuring out a compatible and productive work environment. If an extrovert is asked to sit alone in an office, working on projects all day long, day after day, he or she will feel profound stress. The source of the stress may not be apparent, but forcing extroverts to be non-interactive cuts them off from their most productive work style and causes everything to feel somewhat incomplete and unreal. In the same way, forcing introverts to interact all day long also leads to stress.

Margaret—An Extrovert. Margaret is a sales representative for a large private hospital. She had originally wanted to be a psychologist; but, after earning her master's degree, she realized that being a therapist did not involve interacting freely with people. It involved keeping most of your thoughts to yourself. To be effective, you had to let the patient see just what was good for them to see. Frankly, it drove Margaret crazy. She was never sure what she should say and what she should hold back. She felt she was spending the whole day sitting on her hands.

As a sales representative for a psychiatric hospital, however, she was in her element. Her training and degree gave her credibility; she obviously knew what she was talking about. But her job now asked her to call on companies and insurance providers who were important sources of potential business for the services of the hospital. As Margaret saw it, her job was to form relationships with key people in these companies—people who would know her, remember her, and call her when they were thinking about something the hospital could do for them.

Margaret loves this job. She likes talking to people all day long; she likes knowing them; and they like her. When she has a meeting with someone important, getting to know this person, getting to like him or her, and getting that person to like her occupies her primary attention. She can spend an hour and a half at lunch with an important client and never mention the hospital. Because of her ability to connect, Margaret has been successful at her job—and happy.

Mark—An Introvert. Mark is a corporate consultant. He has a Ph.D. in industrial psychology and has been in practice 15 years. He has two partners, both of whom are Ph.D.'s. He likes to start his day by drinking coffee and reading the paper with his office door closed and his phone blocked. After about a half hour, he emerges and begins his work day. He typically works with one or two corporate clients each day, talking to their executives, working with system problems, writing reports, talking to staff. After lunch, Mark likes to close his door and shut off his phone for another half hour or so to recharge for the afternoon. Mark interacts with people all day, except when he is analyzing data or writing reports, but all of his interactions are structured. He is an expert: his clients seek his help, and he provides it. When he has lunch with a client, they mostly discuss the company, its problems, and its future goals. The only time Mark really talks about his personal life is with his wife and with one or two old friends. Mark likes his job. He feels he is very good at it, and it suits him perfectly.

Mark and Margaret are at the two ends of the continuum between introversion and extroversion. They have both found positions in which their personalities are a positive force in their work. Margaret's ability and drive to connect at a personal level make her an exceptionally effective representative. Her sales contacts sense her desire to connect personally. They trust her because she's not trying to hawk the hospital all the time. She wants to know who they are and what their problems are.

Mark's introversion makes him able to assume the rather lonely role of expert. It also has the subtle effect of making him seem more trustworthy to his clients. They feel he will not say anything merely for effect. He means exactly what he says. He never becomes a part of any organization he helps. And that is fine with Mark. He enters an organization, provides his expertise, and leaves.

Introversion and extroversion, like other personality styles, do not in general determine what kind of work a person should do. Rather, they determine how a person goes about doing what he or she does. Margaret and Mark could trade jobs and undoubtedly be effective, but only by going about their jobs in a totally different way.

The next personality dimension, generalist-specialist, is equally important, but not nearly as well known as introversion and extroversion.

GENERALIST-SPECIALIST

If you were to ask 1,000 people in the United States what is the first word they think of when you say "table," about 280 of them would respond, "chair." Other responses, like "lamp," "cloth," or "floor" follow in terms of frequency. Some people, given this same stimulus word, respond with a fundamentally different kind of response: "Dalmatian," or "clock," or some equally idiosyncratic response. When asked the connection, they reply with something highly personal. "When I sit at my dining room table, my dog, a Dalmatian, always comes over and lies down at my feet."

This observation forms the core of the difference between specialists and generalists. Generalists comprise about 75 percent of the population. They are the ones who answer, "chair." The defining characteristic of generalists is their gut-level understanding of how other people respond to things around them. They understand because they respond to things the same way. When generalists are in meetings, they don't need to worry about whether participants have arrived at consensus. They know. All they have to do is check their gut reactions. Generalists have a clear sense of what is going on with other people. This makes the generalist brilliant at understanding, motivating and leading other people in organizations. The generalist functions supremely well in groups, teams and systems.

The specialist is a different breed. The highly personal and idiosyncratic response noted above is how the specialist goes about life. It's important for specialists to own what they do—almost completely. The name *specialist* refers to their long-observed tendency to find a particular area of knowledge and pursue that one subject for an entire career. In organizations, specialists do not generally fair well. In fact, a true specialist is like an interplanetary alien who has somehow stumbled into the organization's world. If specialists do make it in an organizational structure, it is because they have found some particular area of expertise that is necessary to the system's functioning and have somehow managed to stick with that one particular specialty. They concentrate on that one area until they know more about it than anyone else. They rise in organizations because their special area of knowledge is crucial. What generally happens, of course, is that a specialist who is really performing well and who probably loves what he or she is doing will get promoted. At this point specialists lose that vital personal connection to their jobs that makes them want to get up in the morning. When this happens, they frequently become depressed and dispirited, frequently without knowing why.

Specialists and generalists have two fundamentally different views about work. When you ask a generalist what he or she does at work, you are very likely to hear about a big picture. The company produces this; the team is working on that product; the department is moving in a new direction. The reason generalists function so well in organizations is that they can see what they are doing in terms of an overall result that is the product of many people working together toward a common end. They don't fundamentally care whether they are doing this piece of the work or that piece of it; they mainly care that the team or organization is doing what it set out to do, and that they are rising comfortably in the organizational hierarchy.

Specialists are concerned with what they, personally, are doing. When you ask specialists what they do, they tell you about the element of the particular project that they are personally working on. It's the only thing that makes any real difference to them. Specialists often have a real passion for what they do; that's what makes them so competent in the areas they have chosen.

Joseph, the lawyer we talked about in Chapter Four who was managing partner of his law firm, but unhappy with it, was unsuited by abilities to be a manager. He was also unsuited because, like many lawyers, he was a specialist. He couldn't care less about the overall organization of the firm or the direction it was moving; he just knew he could manage deals with his clients better than anyone on the planet, and that's what he wanted to do.

Specialists tend to populate professions like medicine, accounting, law, and dentistry. These professions have defined areas of expertise, and practitioners function within these areas for their entire careers. They tend not to be parts of large business organizations. If they do form professional groups out of financial necessity, these groups are best described as collections of independent practitioners. Artists, writers, actors, teachers and performers are mostly specialists also. Again, these are people who get ahead because they completely own what they do.

David—A Generalist. David is a manager in an international technology company. He has been on the sales side for many years. He sees his job as motivating his people. At this he is a master. He supports them, pushes them, moves them, finds the right roles for them, or helps them move on to a better fit if they can't find a good role with him. He has been a top producer for years, but is somewhat bemused by this. "I love to get the right person in the right job. I seem to know just how to get people moving and involved in what they are doing, but it's not something anyone taught me. It's like I've always known it. As far as what I know, I know a little about a lot of things. People who work for me know a lot more about their areas than I do. That's fine with me. They love this stuff, but I leave it as soon as I walk out the door."

David is an extrovert with a manager's ability profile. He is the quintessential manager. Recently he was transferred to production. This is fine with David; what he does won't change. Like most generalists, he sees progress in his career in terms of the organization's structure. Production will be a useful springboard upward in the company. This is quite unlike the specialists who often work for David; they see progress in terms of exercising more control over the one job they want to do.

Specialist-generalist is an extremely important dimension in envisioning a career. Asking a specialist to be a manager is an organizational bad joke. Lacking that gut instinct about others that is the defining characteristic of generalists, specialists often do not have a clue about how to motivate anyone. Basically, they have never seen motivation as much of a problem. *They* are motivated. Isn't everyone? Specialists' leadership style, when effective, could be called charismatic. The specialist believes totally in his or her mission and gathers people around who believe, too. These "believers" are usually generalists.

Specialists' defining characteristic of owning what they do makes them generally lousy managers. "Do it my way. This is my project, so don't screw it up. Here, let me show you how to do it. Just do it like I tell you to. I'll do it." These are all utterances of specialists, and utterances that would probably never even occur to a strong generalist. A team of specialists working on the same project (or more likely, on their personal pieces of the same project) can be a beautiful study of accomplishment and efficiency—as long as a manager is in charge. Could the atomic bomb have been built by scientists alone? Not without General Groves.

Interestingly, the reverse problem of generalists landing in "specialist" jobs does not come up very often. Given any choice in the matter, most true generalists aren't that interested in specialists' jobs. They would feel pigeonholed and limited; leave that for the experts. If, by some happenstance, a generalist does land in a specialist job, he or she will almost always go about it differently. Generalists in the professions, for instance, tend to become involved in the organization of the profession—in the professional societies or the state regulatory boards. That's fine with the specialists, because they aren't interested in that stuff anyway.

In the Thought Experiment, you will find a short self-report questionnaire designed to give you a sense of where you fall on the two dimensions of personality we discussed here: introvert-extrovert and generalist-specialist. Taking both of these dimensions into account will give you a picture of the kind of work environment in which you will feel most at home. There is also a short interpretive section so that you can see what the results of the questionnaire mean for you.

A NOTE ABOUT ANXIETY

At this point in the process of creating a Personal Vision, when you are looking at all the pieces, and trying to put a picture together of what you want your career to look like, most people start getting anxious. At the beginning of this process, people make fascinating discoveries about themselves. They discover new talents they didn't know they had before, or didn't know the meaning of. They look at themselves in new and unexpected ways. They reexamine assumptions that they didn't even realize they were making.

So where does the anxiety come in? You may have all sorts of new information, but it's hard to tell yet where it's all going. There's no picture yet. You can't know yet what it all really means. "I keep adding new bits of information and new insights, but where is it all leading?" Intellectually, you may know clearly that this is a big job that will take a while to figure out, but you may still feel anxious now.

We know that this anxiety is an important part of the creative process of building a Personal Vision. When you start feeling this anxiety, you know that *both* parts of your mind, the left and right hemispheres, are engaging fully in the problem of how to put all of this information together. It is as though your unconscious, creative mind is worrying the problem, turning it over, pushing it this way and that, trying to figure it out. Your logical, linear, problem-solving left brain wants an answer. And it knows that it can't provide one.

Researchers who study creative people with the idea of delineating the process of creativity itself invariably comment on this anxiety. The first stage of the creative process involves information gathering and logical attempts at solutions. As the problem starts to take shape, as the scope and extent of it become more clear, the creative person starts to feel anxiety. It is perhaps the mind's way of prodding itself to make a creative leap. This is the beginning of the second stage of the creative process.

The only thing to do is to trust yourself. And keep plugging away at the problem. You need three more pieces to your Personal Vision—values, goals, and family of origin. Then you will be ready to start integrating them and forming your Personal Vision.

THOUGHT EXPERIMENT D:
Skills, Interests and Personality

1. UNCOVERING YOUR SKILLS

You will have to trick yourself to take a fresh look at your skills. You will need a tape recorder so that you can record one or two stories about yourself.

Think of an event in your life when you were younger, one that you feel positive about in retrospect. Think about what happened right before and right afterwards. Think about what you *felt*, what you *did*, and what *happened*. This can be a small event that would only be meaningful to you, or it can be a bigger event that anyone would recognize as positive.

Now tell the whole story into the tape recorder. Be sure to include details of what led up to it, what you did, what you felt, what happened next, how other people responded, and how they felt.

Now record a different story, again one from when you were younger. This time, make it a story about an event which you found frustrating or disappointing. Be sure to include the same details as in the first story.

Now leave your stories for at least two weeks. Don't listen to them, or even think about them if you can help it. When the two weeks are up, listen to the stories again. If it helps, pretend they are about someone else's past. In your notebook, as you listen, write down every positive skill you hear in the stories. Many people write down 15 to 20 different skills in even a simple story. Even in the negative story, be sure to find and write *positive* skills. You may find that you see the same positive skills in both stories.

If you get stuck trying to find positive skills in your stories, give them to someone else to listen to and find skills in them.

What skills appear in both stories?

Are there themes? Do your skills fall into natural groups?

How would you name these groups?

2. FINDING YOUR INTERESTS

Start an Interest File: Get a file folder or a box and put it someplace where you'll see it. Use your box or file to collect notes about anything that gets your attention: articles, pictures, or even random thoughts about what really interests you in life. You don't have to be choosy here. You're not wedded to anything you put in this file; the more you can play with it, the better. What looks like fun? What would really be interesting—even if you don't know anything about it? What would you like to find out more about? What has always fascinated you? Make a note; put it in the file.

Keep Your File at Least a Month: Longer is better. Don't look in it. Just keep putting stuff in. If you are surprised by anything, particularly delighted by something, or if something doesn't turn out the way you were expecting—these are all clues to what you might find interesting. Put a note in your file. Some of the best items are pictures that catch your eye. You don't have to know why it's interesting; just add it to the file.

Don't Try to Make Sense of It Right Away: Give yourself time. This is one of the most important secrets of creativity. Just add to your interest file; you don't have to explain it, justify it, or make sense of it for now. You want to get as wide a sampling as possible of everything that gets your attention all day long. These will be directions in which you are actively being drawn, not just things that you have to do.

After a Few Weeks, Open Up Your Interest File: This is where it starts to be fun. Pull everything out that you have been collecting and spread it out on the floor. Arrange it in piles. Sort out all the items into groups. What interested you about that story? What was fascinating about this picture? How are they related? If you don't get any real groupings, put it all back and keep collecting for a few more weeks. Try again.

Name Your Groupings: Identify some categories for your interests. You need a name for them, because it will help you focus on what you are interested in. Make a list. Put it in order of things that interest you most, if you want to.

Compare Your Interest Groupings with Your Skill Groupings: Any similarities? Any differences? What important skills would you definitely include in your Personal Vision? What interests?

3. SELF-REPORT OF TWO PERSONALITY DIMENSIONS

Read each item and then use the scale below to indicate how accurately the statement describes you. Write your answer in your Personal Vision notebook.

Not at all like me		Mostly not like me		Sometimes yes, sometimes no			Some-what like me		Exactly describes me
1	2	3	4	5	6	7	8	9	10

1. At parties or in social groups, I like to find one person and talk to him or her.
2. People have a hard time knowing what I feel about things.
3. I would prefer reading a good book to going to a party.
4. I give a good deal of thought to things before I say them.
5. I have one or two very close friends, as opposed to a great many acquaintances.
6. I often initiate conversations with strangers when we are thrown together.
7. Sometimes I don't really know what I think about something until I talk it over with someone.
8. I find parties and social gatherings relaxing most of the time.
9. I like to work around others all day.
10. People usually know what I'm feeling.

11. I like working on my own particular projects.
12. It makes me nervous to delegate anything.
13. I don't like working on teams as well as I like working on my own project.
14. I have some specific areas of interest and expertise.
15. I have my own particular way of going about things.
16. When given a task, I try to figure out who can do it best.
17. I like working on a project with others. I'm a good team player.
18. It usually doesn't matter to me what part of a project I take, as long as I contribute to the overall goal.
19. It wouldn't matter too much to me to be transferred to another set of responsibilities.
20. I enjoy the thought of working with other people on a project.

To develop a score for yourself:

I. Add your scores together for items 1-5, 6-10, 11-15 and 16-20 (four separate scores in all).

II. With your totals for items 1-5 and 11-15, subtract each total from 50. If your total for items 1-5 was 10, you would subtract this from 50, yielding a score of 40.

III. Add your score for 1-5 (subtracted from 50) to your score for 6-10. Add your score from 11-15 (subtracted from 50) to your score for 16-20.

IV. Your total score for items 1-10 is for the introvert-extrovert dimension.

V. Your total score for items 11-20 is for the specialist-generalist dimension.

VI. On the introvert-extrovert dimension, rate yourself as follows:

    A. Score: 10-44, Introvert, Paragraph A below.

    B. Score 45-65, Combination introvert-extrovert, Paragraph B below.

    C. Score 66-100, Extrovert, Paragraph C below.

VII. On the specialist-generalist dimension, rate yourself as follows:

    A. Score 10-44, Specialist, Paragraph D below.

    B. Score 45-65, Combination specialist-generalist, Paragraph E below.

    C. Score 66-100, Generalist, Paragraph F below.

INTROVERT-EXTROVERT

Paragraph A: Introvert.

As someone who exhibits Introversion, you get energy and renewal from time spent by yourself. You can learn to be quite adept at social situations and very skillful at handling interactions with others. You must always keep in mind that no matter how skillful you become, there is always the element of work to interactions with others. Long periods of social or business interaction, no matter how satisfying or enjoyable, will always leave you feeling somewhat drained.

On the positive side, Introverts are able to concentrate on tasks that require solitary effort for long periods of time without undue stress. You can handle social situations by learning to be skillful and adept with them, and this means you can be with other people with very little stress provided you allow yourself enough time alone to regenerate.

Paragraph B: Combination Introvert-Extrovert.

You report some characteristics of Extroverts and some characteristics of Introverts. In general, this position on the scale means that you have more choice about your interpersonal environment.

You have a good intuitive understanding of social situations and you enjoy interaction with other people. You are able to listen well to others and guess easily what they are feeling. On the other hand, you are able to be alone some of the time and enjoy this. You are able to concentrate on tasks that can only be done by one person, and not feel too much stress from this. Obviously, the two sides are somewhat incompatible. You will probably find that you lean more in one direction than the other. However, your score indicates that you participate to some extent in both.

You will probably need to allow a good balance in your life between being with others and being by yourself. If you are around people interacting for extended periods, you will probably feel some renewal by being alone. If you are alone for extended periods, you will probably find yourself wanting to be with others.

Paragraph C: Extrovert.

You get energy from being with people and you like being around others through a good part of the day. If you were to get into a job that required you to be alone most of the time, or in which your interactions were so stereotyped that you could not really relate to others, you might well find it stressful and unsatisfying. The reason for this is that you would not be having enough contact with other people in the day.

You have excellent intuitive understanding of social situations and you enjoy interaction with other people. You are able to listen well to others and guess easily what they are feeling. Many people who exhibit Extroversion use interactions with other people to help them understand their own thoughts and feelings. Quite often, a thought or idea does not feel "real" to an Extrovert unless it has been shared with someone else. You will always be happier in a position if you have some way to interact with others.

SPECIALIST-GENERALIST

Paragraph D: Specialist.

Specialists look at the world in a unique way. The Specialist will always see things somewhat differently from anyone else. This is a clear strength in the right setting, and with the right expectations. If you are expected (or expect yourself) to be part of the herd, or to come up with the "regular" response to

THE LEMMING CONSPIRACY

problems, you will always be working against yourself. Your strength is that you may have a different slant on things and a different way of looking at things.

Being a Specialist affects how you perceive others and how you communicate. You tend to like the independence and autonomy that come with having total mastery of a body of knowledge or a skill of your own. Specialists often have clear ideas of what they wish to accomplish, and work with dedication and personal commitment.

Paragraph E: Combination Specialist-Generalist.

You report characteristics of both Specialists and Generalists. Specialists like coming up with original answers to most problems and making unique contributions. Generalists are expert in judging how others in a group respond and contribute. You may well be able to do both to some extent.

You probably enjoy being an expert and having an area of expertise that fascinates you. If you can make this part of your job, it can be a tremendous benefit to you. You are also able to work effectively with teams and groups. This dual characteristic can be extremely valuable in corporations. You can gain a definite position or specialty, but also work effectively in the team atmosphere needed in most business environments.

Paragraph F: Generalist.

Generalists like to work with people and through people. The Generalist usually thinks in terms of the overall goals of the organization, rather than strictly in terms of his or her own specific area or job. A true Generalist can move easily from job to job, and often does, just as long as he or she is furthering the goals of the team. The Generalist does not constantly live and breathe the job, like the Specialist. For the Generalist, the job is a tool, like a hammer, to be picked up and used for an end, and then laid aside when it is over.

Generalists like being part of a team. They are able to think broadly about the overall functioning of the organization, and

133

not be so bound to one particular specialty. A Generalist can be willing for others to have their areas of specialty and expertise, because that can help the team. Whereas the Specialist operates through a particular area of expertise, the Generalist operates through the group.

Four Stories: Skills, Interests and Personality

Tracy

Skills: "I told a story about organizing a paper-recycling project at my high school when I was a freshman. The school, of course, produced reams of paper every day, and they just threw it into the landfill. I thought, 'We can do something about this.' I got about 10 or 12 people in my class to come over on several Saturdays and we made boxes. Then we got all the teachers to put paper in the boxes. Then we organized collection and got a recycling service to pick it all up. I've always done that. I just look around and think, 'What needs to happen here?' and then set out to do it. I could have told a dozen other stories about things I did in high school and college both. I think when I really feel passionately about something, I am good at getting others interested, too."

Interests: "I've always been interested in the natural world and the environment. The pictures and articles I cut out to put in my file were about everything under the sun, but it always kept coming back to animals, the environment, nature, science."

Personality: "I am half-extrovert and half-introvert. No surprise. I like people, but I like being by myself to think every once in a while, too. What was interesting was that I am a total specialist. There have always been *some* things that really interested me. What I enjoy most is going into those subjects totally. There are some subjects I've been interested in for years. I guess that's another reason I don't like my job very much at the law office. I just have to do whatever they tell me to; I don't ever get to have a project or something that's just *mine*."

Feelings now: "I'm getting more excited. I'm seeing more patterns here. I don't know where it's going yet, but I think it's going *somewhere*."

Brian and Janet

Brian's Skills: "When I was a kid, my mother would have garage sales. She always liked me to help her because I was so good at getting people to buy stuff. I could always find exactly the right thought to bring someone around who was wavering about buying. I enjoyed the puzzle: What does this person want? How can I say it so he will want to buy it?"

Interests: "My interests are mostly in people or sports. I like to read about people who are *doing* things. I like interesting ideas. It's intriguing to me to see a particularly well-done print ad. I like to scope out how it catches my attention, and then what it promises. I'm always interested in how you 'hook' people."

Personality: "I am a total extrovert and generalist. It's like I was born knowing people and what makes them do what they do. Put me in a room full of people, and I'm not really happy until I have gotten around to all of them to find out what they think about things."

Feelings now: "Confident. It's amazing how much better I feel knowing how well my job fits me."

Janet's Skills: "The story I told was about doing a senior thesis in college. The school required a thesis for graduation, and most of the other seniors dreaded it. I got interested in the economics of political reform in nineteenth-century England. It was fascinating once I got into it. It combined a lot of different disciplines—history, politics, economics, law—and I had to learn about all of them. Then I had to turn it around and make it understandable to others. I had a great major professor. He kept saying that I knew more about some of this than he did. I got high honors, and he said I should publish it."

Interests: "I really love detective novels. I probably read one or two a week. I like to figure them out before the hero does. I also like reading the news. I like to try to figure out what is really going on. When the president or the treasury secretary says something, I like to predict what the reaction will be in the press."

Personality: "I am a complete introvert, and half-specialist, half-generalist. The introvert part is right. I *like* people, but just one at a time. When I go home, I like to read a book. When I got my scores, I showed them to Brian and said, 'See, that's why I don't like to go around and talk to everyone every time we go out.' I like having one friend, or two. The specialist-generalist score is interesting. Maybe I would like my job better if I weren't feeling pulled in all different directions all the time."

Feelings now: "Very interested. This is fascinating—the same themes keep coming back from the different exercises. Hopeful."

Elizabeth

Skills: "My story was about my senior year in high school. I was president of three organizations and a member of about six others, including cheerleaders. I made good grades, too—almost straight A's. The story really wasn't about all those accomplishments. It was more about how I handled stress. My day was going to meetings, classes, talking to my friends, more meetings, study, talk to my friends, a little sleep. I don't remember feeling tired or stressed, but I can hear my mother's voice, 'Honey, you don't have to do *everything*.' I guess my life's always been the same. Too much to do. Always on the edge of falling apart."

Interests: "I'm interested in my child. I'm interested in

day care. Almost everything in my interest file had to do with child rearing or day care for children. There is so much that could be done with effective day care, but it is almost a total wasteland. Think of what really good day care would mean to lower-income families. I get so angry when I go pick up Frederick, my son, because half the time he's just sitting in front of a television. It's not the day care's fault, though, they don't have any budget."

Personality: "In personality, I'm mostly a generalist and mostly an extrovert. I've always liked working with people in groups. My managerial style is collegial. I like everyone on the team to take an active part in decision-making. I like everyone to feel they have had a say in what happens to them. I have to say, though, that things usually go the way I think they should. As a team, we've been working together for a long time. We don't have much wasted effort. We're the top producer in the division."

Feelings: "Hopeful. I feel like everything I learn adds a new piece to a puzzle. I just want to see what the next piece will add."

Carl

Skills: "I told a story about volunteering at the Free Clinic at my church after I got laid off. For about one day, they had me sorting out donated pills and bandages. Then they put me in charge of organizing the pharmacy. Now I'm organizing the whole volunteer schedule. It has always worked like that with me."

Interests: "I've gotten a lot more interested in my wife and two boys. I have one son who will graduate from college this year, and another who is married and will have a child soon. Since I've been off work, I talk to my sons every week. I try to go over to see the one living in town. It's interesting to find out what they think about things. I'm also interested in the Free Clinic. I think that's a really worthwhile thing to do."

Personality: "In personality, I'm a complete generalist and more extroverted than introverted. I like organizations and teams of people. I like working with them and getting them all moving in the same direction. I know I'm good at that."

Feelings now: "A little impatient. I am finding out a lot about myself, but it doesn't feel new or different. I still don't know where a job is going to come from. I feel I had a pretty good fix on my talents and so forth before."

NEXT CHAPTER: In the next chapter, we start to give your Personal Vision more coherence. Your natural talents are the foundation. Your skills, interests and personality lend it substance and structure. But your values and goals give real life to your Personal Vision.

CHAPTER 6

Giving Life to Your Personal Vision:
VALUES AND GOALS

WHAT ANIMATES A PERSONAL VISION? VALUES AND goals, the subjective factors, shape your Personal Vision—sometimes more than objective factors for those at mid-life or beyond. Values are a sort of road sign that points out a direction; goals are the specific stepping stones on the path to your Personal Vision.

In the process of creating a Personal Vision, identifying your values and goals propels the difficult leap from the Stress Cycle to the Balance Cycle. You may remember from Chapter Two that the Stress Cycle is outer-directed, motivated by wealth and status, focused on short-term issues, and reactive. In the Stress Cycle, you never stop; you just jump through the next hoop. To be in the Balance Cycle, you must have an *interior* sense of who you are and what you want in life. We have discussed the foundation and building blocks: abilities, skills, interests and personality. They are the objective elements of Personal Vision. However, to grapple with your values and goals, you must look at your life from the inside and find out what directs and animates your life—what gives your life meaning.

To grapple with values and goals, you must also look at time. This chapter examines two different kinds of time. With values, the day-to-day time you spend living out your immediate life determines how "in sync" you feel with yourself. To look at goals, however, you need to look into the future—10 and even 20 years ahead.

A QUESTION OF VALUES

Values are one of the most common sources of stress for people between the ages of 38 and 45. Increasingly, as we reach the invisible mid-point of our lives, as we start looking ahead and seeing a limit, we start wondering if what we do all day long is *worth* doing.

Most people do not have this question while they are raising children. Time, energy and money spent towards launching children into the world seem well spent to most people. By mid-life, though, people can see the end of raising children. The question arises, *what now?* What is going to seem equally worth my energy and time?

This is not a trivial question. Answering it can prolong your life, increase your joy and energy, and move you a long way toward *meaning*—that ineffable commodity that separates the living from the waiting-to-die. Even the business world, ever concerned with the bottom line, has begun to recognize that employees who pay attention to their values are more productive. When people's minds *and* hearts are involved in what they do, they perform more fully. They are more involved in their lives and work.

Anne's Story

Anne, 45, was an executive in an international public relations firm. She started with this firm after college and moved steadily upward. She had transferred from the New York to the San Francisco office and had achieved a number of prominent successes. She was "second chair" on the new business team—the vital group of high performers that routinely made pitches to new clients. Anne was married, with two children. One would start college next fall, and the other would follow the next year.

"I couldn't imagine doing anything else. Everything seemed to be going just the way I had planned when I was 25. I liked my job. I could see a path upward. I liked the other people I worked with."

Something had been nagging at her, but she could not articulate what. "I basically just wanted to see if I was missing anything or if there were some other way to go with my career. I knew I wanted *something*, but I didn't know what."

In following a structured process to gain a Personal Vision, Anne discovered why she was so successful in her role in public relations. An extrovert and a specialist, she was a natural performer who liked painting a vivid, compelling picture for clients of the world as she saw it, bringing them in, and letting them see it the way she did. With high Classification and high Concept Organization, she was able, in flashes of insight, to understand and overcome a prospective client's objections to a pitch. Then, using an inexorable tide of logic, she turned the client to her point of view. For her, public relations was perfect.

In the course of discovery, Anne examined influences from her family of origin. In the next chapter, we will talk about the kind of work she did. Her mother and father had been missionaries. Anne had lived a large part of her first 14 years in China. She had absorbed an important value as a child, powerfully communicated by both of her parents: "You should give something back to the world."

Her family did not present this value as a mere homily. When she interviewed her mother and father, Anne discovered that her father, shortly after marrying, had spent two or three years working for a bank as a manager-trainee. He was dissatisfied, though, and at age 25 entered a seminary. He was assigned a small church, but applied to be a missionary because he felt the need was greater. He and his family moved to China when Anne was only two years old. He felt that quitting the bank and embarking on this risky venture that never paid him quite enough made his life feel more vibrant and worthwhile.

Hearing her father and mother's story, some of it for the first time, put many of Anne's nagging doubts into sharper focus. "Public relations was right for me, but I started to see how helping large clients sell more product was not going to be enough. I want to feel that I am contributing more actively to society."

Some months after completing work on her Personal Vision, a memo came across Anne's desk. An international relief agency was looking for someone to be director of public relations. Pay was roughly half of what Anne took home from her present job. "Normally, I would ignore a memo like this. If I knew someone who was looking for a job, I would pass it along. Otherwise, it would go into the trash can."

This time she didn't throw it away. "As soon as I saw it I began thinking about giving something back to the world and how important that had become to me. I went home and discussed it with my husband. We thought that with my savings from bonuses over the years we would not have a difficult time putting our kids through college. Otherwise, our two salaries should be fine."

Anne applied for and got the job. She is now director of public relations for the relief agency and routinely travels all over the globe. "I'm now doing work that is inherently meaningful. It makes use of all of my abilities *and* my experience and skills. It makes everything I've done up to now make sense."

To make values work for you, you must compare your strongest values—what you personally hold most meaningful in life—to how you actually spend your time. That is what Anne did.

Like many people, Anne had never taken the time to articulate clearly her most important values. Articulating values requires a disconcerting shift of focus from the outside to the inside. Anne, like most people her age, had spent the majority of her career jumping through hoops. She had gone after a college degree, a good job, a better position, more pay, a path to the executive suite. Each of these goals had focused her entire attention and energy *outside* of herself.

Let us be clear. None of the hoops Anne so competently jumped through were wrong in and of themselves. What blocked Anne was her failure to look inside to express what would be most meaningful for *her*. All of her goals were set by her systems. She never stopped to question them or decide how they matched up with her profoundest beliefs. She was a victim of the Lemming Conspiracy.

For Anne, the trip inward started when she interviewed her parents. As we shall see in Chapter Seven, there are many positive reasons for interviewing your parents. Without question, it is one of the most powerful things you can do for yourself as an adult. Our values originate in our families of origin. We absorb them fully before we even start school. The most important values are the ones our parents live out—not the values they speak to us in words. This holds equally true for ourselves.

You can clarify your values initially without your family of origin. The Thought Experiment at the end of this chapter will help you articulate what values pull you most strongly. You can use this information to see how your priorities match up with how you spend your time.

What troubled Anne was that once she had a clear sense of her most important values, she realized she did not invest any of her time into living them out. In working with values, we start by establishing priority. What is your most important value? What is next?

The critical and difficult question is this: How do you spend your time? How do you actually live your days? A value, even a dearly held one, feels fundamentally hollow unless you act upon it in real time in your real life. The second part of the exercise in the Thought Experiment helps you compare your most important values with how you spend your time.

Having a fundamental value to live a healthy life and take care of your physical body may be important to living a balanced life. But having this value will do nothing unless you translate it into time. Having health as a primary value, but not spending any time in exercise in a normal week creates a continual disjunction between your values and your life. It is this kind of disjunction that leads to the "hollow men" of the modern world, people who live lives of no meaning to themselves.

In coming to grips with values, we have begun to accumulate enough objective and subjective information to move from stress to balance. In the next section we show how goals form the concrete stepping-stones leading out of the Stress Cycle and into the Balance Cycle. Goals create this path *only* if you link them to all of the information, objective and subjective, you have been gathering about yourself. Once again, as with values, time is the medium through which goals move.

WHOSE GOALS? YOURS OR YOUR SYSTEMS'?

The Lemming Conspiracy insidiously blinds us to the difference between our systems' goals and our own goals. Anne, in the story above, felt absolutely sure she was charting her own course in life. She had a plan; she was following it; and she was on schedule. The nagging doubts she felt at odd moments didn't stop her. In fact, nothing stopped her. As we have seen, *stopping* is the one thing the Lemming Conspiracy will not let you do. The Lemming Conspiracy keeps you grinding away at the Stress Cycle without ever looking up to see what else you might want to do with your life.

Anne assumed her goals were her own. But when she examined these assumptions, she realized that her goals had nothing to do with her most deeply held values. She had left that part of the equation out. Her goals did not reflect who she really was.

As it happened, Anne's goals were a close match for her natural abilities. They took into account her many skills and interests, as well as capitalizing on her interpersonal style. In many ways, Anne's goals fit perfectly, but in one crucial area they missed. In this section, we will talk about how to match your goals to what you know about yourself. The closer you match your goals to all aspects of yourself and what you want out of life, the closer you move to a Personal Vision and the Balance Cycle.

We designed the Thought Experiment at the end of this chapter to help you articulate your goals. What do you want to accomplish in the next five years? Ten years? Expand your goals beyond the limits of work. Your life is bigger than work. What do you want to accomplish in regard to your family? Your friends? Your spiritual life? Your physical self? All of these critical elements enliven and enrich your life just as much, or at times more, than work. Later, as you move toward integration, the difference between your own goals and your systems' goals becomes increasingly apparent.

Over time, you may change some of your goals, eliminate some of them, or add others. It is important to start where you are now. Don't expect yourself to get to answers on the first try. We know from experience that you can't create a Personal Vision from logic alone. There are too many competing pieces to this puzzle. Attempting to pin down your goals is an important preliminary step to the creative work of integrating a Personal Vision.

GOALS THAT CAN BE ACHIEVED—ONE WAY OUT OF THE STRESS CYCLE

Goals are the smaller way stations on the path to a Personal Vision. But some goals can keep you fixed in the Stress Cycle, while other goals can move you away from stress and toward the Balance Cycle. As you might imagine, goals that originate in your systems keep you enmeshed in the Stress Cycle. Goals that originate from *you* create stepping-stones toward a more balanced life.

"I want to be comfortable financially." "I want to be healthy." "I want to be a good father." These sound like fine goals; it's hard to argue with any of them. But as stated, they are not goals at all. They are really more like value statements—a statement about what is important to you. As goals, however, they don't work, because they are *endless*. They must be more clear to help you. You need to know 1) how to know a goal is reached, and 2) when you want to finish it.

SETTING GOALS YOU CAN ACCOMPLISH

For the goals above, what does "comfortable" mean? How much money? When? What does "healthy" translate to in terms of behavior? How many workouts per week? How long? Or what does it mean in terms of blood pressure or cholesterol level? By when? What does "good father" mean for you? Time with your children? How much? How often? How will you know you have succeeded?

Goals are tricky. We tend to feel that once we name a goal, we're done with it. When you deal with goals that might or might not actually be your systems' goals, it is trickier still. One way to recognize a goal that is your systems' rather than your own is that you can never know when you achieve it.

As an example, look at the goal of being financially comfortable. This is a worthy goal, and an important one for anyone in our society. But what does it mean? For most people, there is no end point to this goal. It just means *more*: more money, bigger house, better car, better job. This is a system goal. It pins you in the Stress Cycle.

To make it your goal instead of your systems', you have to translate it into concrete terms for your own life. What are you going to use money to buy? Retirement, house, car, education for your children, security? You can connect an amount of money to each. You can figure out how much and what is enough.

Next, you need to think about *when* you need money. When is retirement for you? When do your children need educational money? These questions may sound obvious and trivial, but they are not. Most people do not ever bother to figure out what is *enough* money. As a result, most are like rats on a treadmill, endlessly running and never getting anywhere.

As we saw earlier in Anne's story, a critical piece of her being able to do what she wanted to do with her life was sitting down with her husband and figuring out what money they needed to accomplish their goals. Before she did this, she had never considered the question, "What would be enough?" But without this step, she would never have made the change she made without feeling anxious about it. As it happened, figuring out and agreeing with her husband on what amount of income would be enough for them was an enormously freeing act. It allowed her to pursue her Personal Vision and change her life for the better.

GOALS AND TIME

The second part of making a goal yours instead of your systems' is putting it on a time line. You have to know not only *what* you want to accomplish, but *when*. In the Thought Experiment, you will see an example of a time line. There are only two ways to go with time: forward and backward. In thinking about goals, it is often most useful to go backwards. Start with what you want to accomplish. Put it on the time line. Then start to fill in behind. In order to accomplish *this*, what else will I need to accomplish? When? Put that on the time line. As you keep working on your time line, it can become an important working document for your career. It should never be static. To make it live and breathe, refer to it; update it; add to it. This can become an important part of your written plan for your life.

SYSTEMS' GOALS VS. GOALS THAT INTEGRATE

Besides being unachievable, another sure sign of a system goal is one that is single-dimensional. "I want to earn $1,000,000 before I'm 50." You clearly know if you accomplish this. You know when you want to accomplish it. But is it a system goal, or yours?

It is totally one-dimensional. If a client were to state a goal like this, we would ask, "Why?" The answer might have something to do with power, prestige, things he or she could buy. These are goals that leave people in the Stress Cycle. They don't lead anywhere and don't really have anything to do with the person, only with his or her systems.

On the other hand, the answer could have something to do with security, children, or the ability to tackle a life-long ambition. This is better. People who answer this way are at least thinking about themselves and what they want from their lives. But in this case, the goal becomes security, or having adequate money to educate children, rather than $1,000,000 before 50. If you address these issues in your goals, you will go a lot further toward moving yourself out of the Stress Cycle.

We talked to a lawyer once, the founding partner of a very successful corporate law firm. He stated his goals this way: "I have spent nearly 60 years amassing a fortune. In a few years, I'll retire, and my goal is to spend it." This lawyer has one of the finest strategic minds in the field. He has made his fortune because he is so adept at keeping his clients out of the very kind of trap into which he has himself fallen. He is a victim of the Lemming Conspiracy. He told us in the same interview that he particularly enjoys working late on Saturday night because no one is in the office to bother him. He is in the Stress Cycle, and his goal will not help him out. His whole universe is bounded by his role as a lawyer. If he is not that, what is he?

Many things. But he won't be able to know that unless he breaks out of the Lemming Conspiracy.

Ideally, all of your goals should relate directly to all or most of the important factors of your life. For instance, as you define what security means for you, how does it relate to your abilities, interests and personality? How does it relate to your skills and experience? How does it relate to your values? To see how all of these factors work together with a person's goals, let us tell you about a young woman with a fairly specific goal—she wanted a job within six months.

Ruth's Story

Ruth had been a buyer of women's clothes for a department store chain for five years when a bigger chain of stores bought her company and she lost her job through restructuring. She had not liked her job very much, finding it stressful and unrewarding, so she wanted a job in a new field. She had no idea where or how to start looking.

Ruth had enough money to live for six months without going too deeply into her savings. At the beginning her goal was simple and straightforward: Get a job, any good job that paid about the same as she had been making, but in a different field, before her savings cushion ran out.

As she found out more about herself, her goals changed. She discovered natural artistic talents of which she had been previously unaware. She also discovered much about her previous job that she liked and that suited her well. She liked the travel and contact with people; she also enjoyed working with different kinds of fabric and cloth. She had always been fascinated by fabric, and had for a time thought about becoming an artist in cloth and natural fiber. She didn't think she could make enough money with this kind of work, however. One aspect of her previous job she did *not* like was the boring kinds of cloth and clothing she was required to handle. As you might imagine, she discovered she was a specialist, so her interest and fascination with cloth made more sense to her. Her dissatisfaction and discomfort in the large organization she had been working for also made more sense.

So her goal became more specific: she wanted a job in an artistic field, with a small company, or perhaps an individual, that involved working with specialized cloth, and that made use of her skills and experience acquired as a buyer. This goal related strongly to her Personal Vision, and encompassed several critical factors she had discovered and wanted to express in her life.

Ruth used a process called Surveying to make her goal real. We will discuss Surveying in more detail in Chapter Nine, and we will talk in detail about how Ruth carried out her Survey project.

In Surveying over four months, Ruth received three job offers that fully met her first criteria: good job, decent pay, different field. But she knew they didn't match her goals; they would not satisfy her in the long run. She turned all three down and pressed on with her Survey. She found this surprisingly easy.

Ruth finally connected with an architect who had an interior design studio. He wanted a person to buy unusual and artistic cloth from Italy and France for his customers wanting something different in their homes. He had been looking for someone to do this for almost a year. Ruth got the job in one interview because she could tell the architect, in detail, exactly how her goals, interests, fascinations, skills, experience and personality worked together to make her perfect for what he wanted her to do. She took this job and is still happily buying cloth.

Ruth's story illustrates several principles we feel are crucial.

1. *The best answers—the ones that lead to the greatest satisfaction in the end—come from inside you.* No counselor, no matter how well educated, administering no matter how many tests, could have advised Ruth to seek and find the job she ended up with. No one else could possibly know enough about her to give her this advice. Her previous employer could not

know; an outplacement service could not know; a career counselor could not know. But Ruth knew. It was always inside her;
it just needed a process to bring it out and make it plain to
Ruth herself.

2. *First finding out about yourself defines and lays out the
most direct and efficient route to finding a satisfying job or a
satisfying fit in your present job.*

3. *If you create a clear goal that includes enough about yourself, and keep that goal in front of you as a target, you can generally find what you are looking for.*

4. *By creating a Personal Vision and using it as a template, you
can know clearly which opportunities to accept and which to
turn down.*

Ruth's initial goal—find a job, any job—was a product of the
Stress Cycle and would undoubtedly keep her in it. By the time
she had turned down three jobs that met her first criteria, she
knew more clearly what she wanted and how that was different
from what her systems would choose for her. Ruth's Personal
Vision, and the goals she developed out of it, allowed her to
break the Stress Cycle and move toward the Balance Cycle.

THOUGHT EXPERIMENT E:
Values and Goals

1. YOUR VALUES AND YOUR TIME

How can you know what's important to you? How can you know if you are out of sync?

Go to the values lists below. Read over the entire list.

Start with the Priority list. Think about the importance of each of the values on the list. What are the most important ones from your point of view? What values do not seem as important?

Now number the values, 1 being most important to you, 2 being next, and so on until you have numbered the entire list of 16 values from the most to the least important.

VALUES LIST—PRIORITIES

(number from 1-16 according to your own priority)
Security
Monetary Success
Family
Position
Wisdom
Health
Stability
Productivity and Competence
Creative and Artistic Work
Spiritual Fulfillment
Authority and Decision-Making
Excitement
Innovation
Physical Challenge
Friendship
Change and Variety

Now go to the Time list. Carefully go through your calendar for the last two months and count up the hours you spent directly working toward each of the values on the Time list. If you spend 10 hours at work each day, for instance, you might count this toward monetary success, position, authority, and/or security, but it would probably not go to family, health, or spiritual fulfillment. Now rank the values on the Time list according to your Time, Energy, and Focus, with 1 being the value toward which you put the most of your actual time, energy and focus, down to 16, where you put the least.

<u>VALUES LIST—TIME</u>

(put number of hours spent directly working on each in last month, rank according to time, energy and focus, 1-16)

Security
Monetary Success
Family
Position
Wisdom
Health
Stability
Productivity and Competence
Creative and Artistic Work
Spiritual Fulfillment
Authority and Decision-Making
Excitement
Innovation
Physical Challenge
Friendship
Change and Variety

Compare the two lists—what you consider your priorities versus where you put your actual time, energy and focus.

If your **high priority values** (1, 2, or 3 on your priority list) are **low time/energy/focus values** (13, 14, or 15 on your time/energy/focus list), this causes stress. This lack of inner direction, of course, is a major function of the Stress Cycle.

In the same way, if your **low priority values** (13, 14, or 15 on your priority list), are **high time/energy/focus values** (1, 2, or 3 on the time/energy/focus list) this also signals disjunction in inner directedness, and also causes stress. Again, as you get older, the stress increases.

Stress due to disjunction between what people hold meaningful and how they actually live their lives tends to force itself into consciousness for the first time at the Mid-Life Transition (age 38-45). However, young people feel this stress, too, even if they are not paying attention to it. The sooner people pay attention to their values and work to bring them in sync with their daily routines, the more alive, productive and enthusiastic they tend to feel about their work.

2. PLACING YOUR GOALS IN TIME

First of all, write down all the goals you can think of in your Personal Vision notebook. Near goals, far goals, personal goals, work goals, family goals, health goals, money goals. Don't worry about grouping them yet.

When you have a significant number of goals covering different aspects of your life and career and different times in the future, start grouping them. Connect ones that go together, creating subsets within categories. You may find that you have a few large goals and that many of the others are smaller goals leading to the larger ones.

In your Personal Vision notebook, draw a line. At the beginning of the line, put your age now. At the end, put 100. Now fill in your Turning Points, every 10 years between the age you are now and 100. Mark ages 40, 60 and 80 with heavy lines, as they tend to be major transition points for most people. Some people use a large poster for this exercise; some people tape several sheets of paper together to create a large foldout in their Personal Vision notebooks. Feel free to create your time line in any way that makes it come alive for you.

Place your major goals on the line at the age you wish to attain them. Feel free to be as creative with this as you want—it's your career, and your time line. Put pictures on your time line if you want to, draw diagrams, use colors. Your line doesn't even have to be straight. If you want hills and valleys, put them in.

After you have your major goals on the time line, fill in the smaller, intermediate goals. Again, let yourself have some freedom to create. Fill up your sheet with goals and connect them to a time line.

As you continue with your exploration and work on your Personal Vision, you might find that you want to change some of your goals, add new goals, or take some goals out altogether. You may find that after you have done the creative Thought Experiments in Chapter Eight, you want to do another time line, taking more of your life into account. The main task is to create a working document that you will be able to use and refer to as you make your Personal Vision real.

FOUR STORIES: VALUES AND GOALS

Tracy

Values: "The values were interesting. My highest values were productivity, excitement, innovation and change. My lowest were security, money, position and stability. All of my *time*, though, is spent holding down a job that's exactly the same drudgery day after day just so I can earn enough money to live on. I'm pursuing my very lowest values with all my time and energy. It's no wonder I feel so discouraged."

Goals: "My most immediate goal is to figure out what I'm going to do next. I've given myself three months. I need to get out of my job at the law firm *yesterday*. Even more than that, I need to be aiming in some direction that will yield some of the excitement and change I want so badly. I want to be *involved* with what I do."

Feeling now: "Determined. Confident. I know more what I'm looking for."

Brian and Janet

Brian's Values: "My strongest values were monetary success, family, competence and decision-making authority. My weakest were artistic work, spiritual fulfillment, physical challenge and health. I guess I would rather watch a game on television with a gang of friends than run or exercise. When I look at my time and energy, it looks about the same, with the exception of family. It's one of my highest values, but I don't put any time into it at all. That bothers me. The health one being on the bottom bothers me, too. I guess I'm just taking health for granted."

Goals: "My goals are these: make the million-dollar club this spring, get at least two older executives to know who I am and be interested in my career, and be in the fast-track pool by next spring."

Feelings now: "Thoughtful. I wonder why I don't want to spend any time or energy toward family."

Janet's Values: "My highest values: family, security, money and stability in that order. I would also put friendship in the highest group. Lowest: position, authority, physical challenge, and change. I think family is really the number one priority for me, but when I look at my time, it's totally different. I don't put *any* time into family. I just work to make money, so that's in line, I guess. But I don't care at all about promotions and getting more authority. I look at the people in charge, and they seem a lot more stressed than I am. They certainly don't seem happy."

Goals: "Have a family, get a different job, or else quit entirely."

Feelings now: "Kind of trapped. Maybe a little confused about what I want."

Brian: "I notice how different we are on our goals. I'm

totally focused on work. Janet is totally focused on family. Most of our values are similar, I think. We both want to have a good lifestyle, and we both feel that family is important. As far as family goes, neither one of us is putting much time into it right now. I don't feel I will ever be able to put much time into it and still reach my goals. So I guess it's nice that it's so important to Janet, because she can sort of make up for me."

Janet: "I'm glad to see that Brian and I have some of the same values. I really see how important family is for me, and how we're not doing anything about it right now. That's sort of worrisome to me."

Elizabeth

Values: "My top values: family, stability, spiritual fulfillment and friendship. I can tell you right now, I'm not putting my time into any of these. They are all pretty much at the end of my time list. My bottom values: monetary success, position, excitement and variety. *These* are what I put my time into. My life is upside down. I have been working, working, working for all the things that I value least. What I value most barely gets any of my actual time."

Goals: "Change this situation. Now. Immediately. I just don't exactly know how. My only option seems to be to quit, and I am not going to do that—yet."

Feelings now: "Mad. Determined."

Carl

"My primary values are family, wisdom, health, position—in that order. Lowest on the list (but not unimportant, certainly) are excitement, innovation, creative and artistic work, and physical challenge. I am spending more time with my wife, and it is very rewarding. I talk to my children regularly. It makes me think about what I missed while I worked so hard for my company. The same with health. I am working out regularly for the first time since college. Maybe this will all make me a little wiser. Actually, the only thing missing from my top values is position, of which I have none, of course. I do work on it every day, but it's discouraging to think that I may have to take less pay and benefits than I had before. One thing I think about is that I don't want to get back into a rat race when I take a new position. I don't exactly know how I would pull that off, but I feel better now than I have in years. I'm closer to my wife, and closer to my children. I don't want that to go away."

Goals: "Get a new job. Soon. I'm beginning to think, though, not just any job I can find. I want it to be one that fits me."

Feelings now: "I can see what I was missing before. I don't want to make the same mistake again. I'm afraid that if I get back into a job, the same forces that drove me to work 60-hour weeks will drive me to do that again. To tell the truth, sometimes I don't really want to go back."

NEXT CHAPTER: In the next chapter, we talk about the final factor you need before integrating all of the factors into a Personal Vision: your family of origin. Just as the Lemming Conspiracy begins in the family of origin, so the family provides by far the greatest energy for breaking out of it. By understanding your family of origin's impact and working with it in a structured way, you may have your best tool for moving your life to the Balance Cycle.

CHAPTER 7

Beating the Lemming Conspiracy with Your FAMILY of ORIGIN

THERE IS NO MORE POWERFUL INFLUENCE ON OUR lives than the family in which we were born and grew up. We form our personalities here, largely before age six. We learn our sense of limits here. We learn what work is and how people go about it. So much of what we learn in the family is unconscious that it is sometimes difficult to know the extent of its influence. Most of our learning about systems takes place as children, and as adults we conveniently forget most of what happened before age six. While we may have no recollection of exactly what we learned, the lessons become part of our emotional and social DNA.

Psychologists may sometimes blame parents or families for much of what's wrong. We have never found this approach to be particularly productive. Figuring out what *positive* things you learned in your family, finding out what makes you unique, and, most of all, asking how your parents made key decisions at Turning Points in their lives moves you into new territory. This new information transforms you and your systems.

Our parents' key decisions at Turning Points form the model for how *we* make decisions at Turning Points. Understanding the how and why of our parents' decisions can help us start to live our own lives instead of reliving our parents'.

Our parents are the source of the most valuable information we can have about ourselves, but tapping into it requires particular effort. Normally, a great deal of the most significant information in families is *not* spoken of. It is "understood," or not seen to be as significant as it is. Often our roles in families come to take precedence over our individual selves. It may be more important for me to be "father" than it is for me to be a living person with hopes, fears, inconsistencies, mistakes, ambitions and ambivalence. Families often don't know how to talk about the most important matters because they never get much practice. It's not through any conscious withholding, but merely from force of habit. We have taught thousands of people in our programs how to return to their families of origin and find out some of the most fascinating and significant information they will ever discover. You can, too.

FAMILIES OF ORIGIN AND THE LEMMING CONSPIRACY

If the Lemming Conspiracy starts in the family of origin, the family of origin also helps us escape it. As we saw in Chapter One, our family systems form the model for all future systems in our lives. We learn how to make decisions at critical junctures in our lives, and we learn how to handle such normal aspects of living as work, disappointment, success, the future, balance and families themselves. None of this learning is conscious. In Chapter One we spoke of the psychological process of *identification*. We absorb our parents, and they remain part of us forever. That's what allows us to function and succeed in the world. Their influence is far more valuable and pervasive than all spoken messages combined in terms of ability to live our lives. But identification with our parents is also what leads us to make errors at Turning Points—decisions about our careers that keep us enmeshed in the Lemming Conspiracy.

Mitchell's Story, continued

We met Mitchell in Chapter One. He had worked in a large technology firm, but found a much better fit for himself in a smaller, more entrepreneurial company. Before he did family-of-origin work, Mitchell unknowingly repeated important decisions his father had made 25 years earlier.

When his father was 30, exactly the same age Mitchell was when he felt so dissatisfied, he worked for a large insurance company. Also dissatisfied, his father wanted desperately to start his own business. But he was newly married and had a small child, Mitchell. After much anguish and soul-searching, he decided he could not make this jump. It was too risky. He continued with the insurance company, buried his feelings, and soldiered on.

But the dissatisfaction came back 10 years later, stronger than ever. When Mitchell's father was 41, he decided to start his own entrepreneurial business. Mitchell remembers this time in the family's life. There was never enough money. His father was never home. His mother exuded stress and anger. Mitchell left for college, and his father continued the business for four more years. But it was never successful and eventually failed. To support his family, Mitchell's father went to work in the insurance agency of an old friend.

Mitchell's father never escaped the Lemming Conspiracy. He ignored his feelings when he was Mitchell's age and kept working for the large insurance company. At mid-life, he made a precipitous jump for which he was unprepared in terms of capital, experience or personality. It was not quite a disaster for the family, but close. He ended up in a job he did not like, far more stuck than he was before, and with an even more limited view of his options.

Even though he didn't know it, Mitchell had absorbed

all of this as a child. As a 30-year-old man with a young family working for a large international company, Mitchell had been successful. Thoughts of starting a business of his own also came to him, and he also rejected them as too risky. He felt trapped and stuck—much like his father at the same age.

At this point, instead of swallowing his feelings, Mitchell embarked on a structured process to create a Personal Vision. He has this to say about his interviews with his father: "It was like a door opening. My father telling me how he had struggled and suffered with this decision was like looking into my own life. I could see that I was set to make exactly the same mistakes that he did—and regretted. It was interesting because his *advice* was: "Don't leave your company." But when I asked him to tell his story and describe why he decided to do what he did, it was clear that he saw only two options: leave or stay. His advice to me was to stay. It was well-meaning and based on his experience of the world, but it was from the same either/or point of view that he saw in his own life. Once I realized that, the clouds began to clear and I decided that there was probably another, middle way that he just didn't consider. Incidentally, it also helped to know that there were reasons I wanted to leave my company and go to a smaller one. It wasn't just some ego-driven, arbitrary wish on my part. It had to do with my natural abilities, personality and interests. There were some *objective* reasons why the fit in my job wasn't right. So in that sense I had an advantage my father didn't."

Mitchell ended up in a smaller, entrepreneurial technology firm. He could make full use of the skills and experience acquired in his previous job, but expand into more areas of interest and take on more roles than he ever would have been able to otherwise. He had at least as much security as he did at the larger company. Even though he did not earn quite as much as before, he felt the new company afforded more long-range potential. For Mitchell it was a good compromise. He had beaten the Lemming Conspiracy.

Mitchell's feelings were almost identical to those of his father's at the same age. He would have, in all likelihood, made the same decision, and for the same reason his father did at that age. And it would probably have been as big a mistake for Mitchell as it was for his father. Mitchell had absorbed his father's limited point of view without realizing it. If he had not asked his father specifically what life decisions he had made and why, Mitchell would have continued operating from this point of view.

Mitchell's story exemplifies all of our lives. We take over the worldview of one or the other of our parents—even when we consciously want to do anything but. All of us absorb information from *both* parents. However, we tend to have a worldview and feelings very much like only one or the other parent—often the parent of the same sex as ourselves. When we change and grow in life, we tend to broaden our behavior and perspective. Often this widening of viewpoint involves allowing information from the other parent to emerge.

When Mitchell took the time to ask and listen to his father talk about his life, many things changed. It was as if he could see his father for the first time. This was not *father*, but a *person*. A person who had been a young man once, just like Mitchell. Who had been anxious and depressed at times, had had a young family once that he wasn't sure he could take care of, who didn't know what the future would bring, and who just took his best shots at life decisions and hoped they were the right ones.

Just as he saw that he and his father were a lot alike and had many similar thoughts and concerns, Mitchell also saw that they were different. One advantage Mitchell enjoyed was that he knew more clearly what he wanted. For another, he saw that he didn't need to be bound any longer by his father's point of view. This freed him to make decisions different from those of his father.

GOING AGAINST SYSTEMS—HOW THE FAMILY OF ORIGIN HELPS

We all live in systems and will continue to do so. No system will voluntarily change. It will keep flowing in the same circular channel—and keep channeling its members into the same roles—unless it is dragged, kicking and screaming usually, into a new channel by someone inside it.

It is obviously difficult to go up against systems, and even more difficult to effect any lasting change. But it can be done. Let us tell you more of Joseph's story. Joseph was the lawyer we met in Chapter Four.

Joseph's Story, continued

Joseph decided not to continue as a managing partner. He had been excellent at that role, from the point of view of his firm. When he became aware of how unhappy he was with the role, he thought about quitting it. But quitting felt momentous, and he knew that many of his partners would be unhappy. He also knew that his wife would question it and be unhappy. She felt his position cemented her husband's influence in the firm.

Joseph felt stuck. He knew *what* he wanted to do, and he knew *why*. It made sense, but it felt like too big a leap. He felt the Lemming Conspiracy's pressure to keep him on track. The system had a role for him; the system provided goals; the system wanted Joseph to continue to see its point of view, not Joseph's.

Joseph interviewed his father about his life and decisions at important Turning Points. His father had been a successful physician in general practice and had done well financially and professionally. He was part of a large group of general practitioners in a city in Texas. He told Joseph that when he was 40, he went through a period of boredom and malaise. The work was always the same. One day he felt that if he saw one more kid with a sore throat and runny nose with a depressed, strung-out, lonely mother he would scream. He went so far as to think about applying for another residency, perhaps in psychiatry. He dismissed it as impractical. It would cost him a lot of money; he had a child, Joseph, getting ready to go to college; he would be giving up a successful practice to start all over again; everyone would think he had suddenly lost his mind. There were a hundred reasons why it wouldn't work. He might not even be able to get into a residency.

Eventually, Joseph's father settled down to his career. He told Joseph that it was soon after this that he had his first affair outside of his marriage. It was with a patient. He had others; sometimes he felt that only this excitement kept him functioning. Now close to retirement, his practice remained busy and profitable, but he felt that perhaps he drank too much. He had no plans other than to keep practicing until he died.

Joseph: "I felt like I had just had a prophetic dream. I could see how my father had struggled with exactly the same feelings I had when he was my age—we both realized our jobs were killing us, even if the reasons were different. He had the same abilities and personality I do, and I could see that he needed the same kind of stimulation in his work that I do. When he gave up trying to get that stimulation from his job, he got it in other ways, ways that he feels badly about now. I don't think he really sees the connection between feeling stultified and trapped at work, and starting to have affairs, but I see it clearly. He wanted his life to be more interesting. Me, too."

When Joseph realized the power of these messages from his family of origin, and when he saw what he knew would be his own future, his vision became clear. He wanted to quit as managing partner—for many good reasons. He wanted to concentrate on work that he enjoyed and that stimulated him, not on work that felt like drudgery. He wanted to be an active presence with his wife and children.

As Joseph became more certain of his ideas, he started letting his wife and partners know what was coming. No one was very enthusiastic, but Joseph's belief and certainty that it was right for *him* carried him through. At first, both his wife and his partners acted as though nothing would happen—until Joseph turned in a letter resigning his role as managing partner. In two months, the person he had chosen to succeed him (*not* the person next in line of seniority; rather, the person Joseph felt had the abilities and personality that fit the job) took over. That day, Joseph left early. He didn't work any more weekends.

Some of Joseph's partners were so mad that they talked among themselves, but when they realized the firm was not collapsing and that revenues were not dropping, everything settled down. Some months later, some of the partners realized that the firm was being run better. Some of Joseph's partners started talking about leaving at six o'clock themselves, and not working so much on the weekends. The system adjusted to new information and became more open.

"It was the same with my wife," Joseph said later. "One day I came home around 5:30 and she was trying to get the kids' dinner ready. She was mad and the kids were hanging on her legs. They were all tired and cranky. I took the kids outside and we shot some baskets while she finished dinner. It was a blast! Sometime later my wife came out and called us all to dinner, but she was obviously angry. I tried to find out why, but she wasn't talking. Finally, later, it all came out. She had had to raise the kids by herself all these years and now I decide to have a mid-life crisis and come home at a decent hour and have *fun* with them and her life is just as boring as ever. Sometimes *she* would like to have a mid-life crisis and do something different. I thought that sounded pretty reasonable."

Joseph is describing systems' reactions to change. First, the system tries to keep roles and relationships the same. If a person in the system tries to change, the system works subtly to move that person back in line. If faced with the threat of real change, systems work more overtly to return things to normal. Sometimes systems exert this pressure crudely and powerfully. Often people in systems feel angry when someone challenges the system's rules. It is important to keep in mind that if you decide that you can have more choices in life than you felt before, this throws a challenge up to *everyone else* in your systems. If you have more choices, then maybe they do, too. Rather than look at that rather frightening thought, sometimes it's easier to convince the errant member that he or she *really doesn't* have any other choices.

For systems the final solution is to reject. Throw the heretic out. Hire someone else who fits. Divorce.

Joseph's systems adjusted.

If a person changes *and* stays, the system must change. It must eventually adjust to the new information. This happened with Joseph's systems. His wife and children adjusted to having a more active and present husband and father. His wife started to take better care of herself. She is now planning to start freelance work in design—a field she had been in before her marriage. Joseph's firm adjusted to a new manager, but more important, it adjusted to the added possibilities Joseph introduced. Partners didn't necessarily have to work until late at night and on weekends; they didn't necessarily have to fail in their marriages.

Joseph's systems became more *open*. That is, they had more options available, and they could be more responsive to new information from the environment. No system is totally open—if it didn't have rules, it would not be a system. Many systems are highly rigid and closed, but all human systems must be at least somewhat open to new information to survive. The most difficult obstacle facing people who want to set their own courses in life is the Lemming Conspiracy—the power of systems to control their thoughts, feelings, and actions—even when it runs counter to self-interest. Once a person has gathered and integrated enough information about himself or herself, once he or she has started to chart a course, it is time to go to the beginning of the Lemming Conspiracy, the family of origin. That is what both Joseph and Mitchell did. This is what you can do.

GOING BACK TO THE FAMILY—WHY? AND HOW?

Both Joseph and Mitchell learned crucial information, instrumental in being able to stand up to pressure from their systems, by interviewing their parents. How does this work? Why would asking your father and mother about what they did and thought when they were teenagers have anything to do with you now? Don't you know that stuff already? And would they talk to you about it, anyway?

Interviewing your parents, if you have done the right preparation, can be a fascinating experience. It can help you to see yourself, and your systems, in a new perspective, one that is outside usual channels.

The most difficult problem you will face in doing family interviews will be setting them up in such a way that you really move *outside* your usual interactions. The interactions must be different to be effective in giving you new information to take back to your systems. In the Thought Experiment, you will see detailed and specific instructions for setting these interviews up and carrying them out. Following them closely can help you break out. This is a situation in which your instincts will naturally lead you into your usual circle of interactions. They will keep you inside the Lemming Conspiracy.

It is also important to be ready for the interviews. It's tempting to feel that if this is the most powerful exercise, then let's just do this one and be done with it. But all that comes before is crucial to conducting your family interviews. Preparation helps you understand what is unique about you and your career.

In interviewing your parents, your goal is to learn to see them as distinct from what your system has taught you to see, and thereby to see yourself distinctly as well. As Joseph remarked, "It was like I saw my mother and father for the first time."

THOUGHT EXPERIMENT F:
Interviewing Your Family of Origin

Undertaking family-of-origin interviews can be a mind-opening, enjoyable experience in which you find out a lot more about two of the most important people in your life. But only if you set it up well. We recommend following all instructions exactly; each one has a definite purpose.

WHOM TO INTERVIEW:

Ideally, you want to interview both of your natural parents in separate interviews, with no one else there besides the two of you.

If you were raised by a stepparent for a significant part of your childhood, you would also want to interview the stepparent. If one or both of your parents is not available for interview, because of death or severe disability, then you should interview a substitute. This could be (in order of desirability) the deceased or disabled parent's brother or sister, close personal friend or cousin, or an older cousin of yours. Failing all of these, your brothers or sisters can substitute. You would conduct this interview just like you would with your parent—asking the substitute about *his* or *her* life, not about your parent's. Only after talking about the substitute's life in detail, just as you would have asked your parent, would you turn to asking what they might know about your parent's life.

WHEN TO INTERVIEW:

After you have done all the Thought Experiments leading up to this one.

HOW TO SET UP THE INTERVIEWS:

Call your mother or father. Let's say you start with your mother. Tell her that you would like to talk with her in about two or three weeks. She would be doing you a great favor and you would like to have the conversation when it would be most convenient for her. You would like to set aside about one or two hours to ask her some questions about her life. You will be coming just to do the interviews, not for any other reason. You won't be bringing anyone else with you.

This sounds simple and straightforward, but it represents a shift *out* of the family system. Some typical responses to this request, and your answers:

What do you want to ask? I just want to find out some things about your life. Sort of like *Roots*—a family history thing.

Why wait two weeks? Let's do it tomorrow. No, I would rather plan ahead so that we can be sure we both have the time put aside. Also, I want to make sure that I have my ideas and questions ready.

Is this going to be some kind of confrontation? Absolutely not. I just want to find out some more about your life. It would be a big help to me.

Will you be bringing your wife/husband/children? No, it will just be me.

Are you going to interview Father? Will you interview us together? Yes, I will definitely interview Father, too. No, I want to interview you separately so I can concentrate on you one at a time.

You should end by saying that you want to be sure you can interview her without being interrupted. Then, talk to your father in a separate conversation and set up the same kind of interview with him.

WHAT YOU TALK ABOUT:

Below are some questions, but you should think of these as starting points. If anything grabs your interest, pursue it. Make sure you ask your parent how he/she *felt* about whatever happened. Also ask for the *reasoning* behind whatever your parent did. What was his/her plan? What was he/she thinking about?

Let's assume we are talking about your interview with your mother again. You can follow the same questions and format with your father.

Usually it's best to start with your mother's parents:
1. What did your father do for work?
2. How did he come to do that?
3. What particular skills or abilities made him good at that?
4. What kinds of things came easily or naturally to your father? [not necessarily work-related]
5. Did he have a hobby or avocation?
6. What did your mother do for work?
7. How did she come to do that?
8. What particular skills or abilities made her good at that?
9. What kinds of things came easily or naturally to your mother?
10. Did she have a hobby or avocation?

Next, you would ask about your mother herself, generally following a time line in your interviews.

Take her back to the age of the first Turning Point in her mind:
1. What was going on when you were 17?
2. Who were your friends?
3. What were you thinking your life would be like?
4. What were you thinking you would do with your life?
5. How did you feel about that?
6. How did you decide what to do immediately after high school? Why?
7. What happened then?
8. What did your parents think about your choices?

For whatever she decided to do (go to college, for instance, or go to work, or get married), ask the following questions:
1. What skills made you good at it?
2. What came easily? What was more of a struggle?
3. What were some problems you encountered? How did you respond?

4. Did you ever wish you had done it differently? How? Why?
5. Describe a bad day. What made it bad?
6. Describe a very good day. What felt rewarding about it?

In this way, go through each major Turning Point of your mother's life listed below. Taking her mentally back to that age, asking questions about what her life was like, what decisions she made, why, and how she felt about them before, during and after.

- High School to College—age 17-18
- College to the Work World—age 22-25
- Age-30 Assessment—age 28-33
- Mid-Life Transition—age 38-45
- Age-50 Assessment—age 50-55
- Pre-Retirement Transition—age 60-65
- Age-70 Assessment—age 70-75
- Senior Transition—age 80-85

You may want to tape-record your interviews. They may be a valuable reference for you or your children.

FOUR STORIES: FAMILY OF ORIGIN

Tracy

"I interviewed both my mother and my father for about three hours each. It was amazing. My mother went to nursing school and met my father when he was an intern in the hospital where she was. She never actually worked as a hospital nurse. She worked in a doctor's office to make money while my father finished his residency, and then to make ends meet when he started a practice. It was a stable job with regular hours, and that's what they needed at the time, since they had a young family. But she hated the routine of it. When she could, she quit, and has never worked since. She's had some problems with depression—especially since the children left home. I sort of knew that was going on, but it felt great to talk to her about it. It turns out, she has been feeling that she *should* do something, work somewhere, but doesn't know what to do, either.

"My father has been like a total force of nature. He still works 12-hour days, just like when I was a kid. He says he has always loved practicing medicine. He gets mad because he says the profession is changing so much. He was really against my going into psychology because he said I'd never be able to make a living. I asked him about retirement. He said he will never retire. Just work until he dies."

Feelings: "It's a little much to put together right now. I can see myself in both of my parents. When I was going strong in psychology, I was just like my father. But then when I lost focus, I became just like my mother, kind of depressed. I can see some problems with some decisions they made, and I could see myself doing the same thing. I can see that I need to have something of my own to sink my teeth in. But I don't want it to be my entire life, like my father."

Brian and Janet

Brian: "My father runs an insurance office in my home town. He has always been pretty successful, though not amazingly so. People like him and trust him, and he keeps customers forever. He had to go out at night a lot. He just felt it was part of the job; he had to do whatever it took. He said he felt like his major duty as a father was to earn a good living and provide for his family. That was what *his* father did. His father lost his business because of the Great Depression. My father said that he never recovered. It just wiped him out—financially and spiritually. He got work again, but he was never the same. I think that left a profound impression on my father. It's like my father said, 'That's never going to happen to me.' I don't get the sense that he has *enjoyed* his life very much.

"My mother was a housewife and took care of me and my two sisters. I don't think she was terrifically happy either, but I felt a lot closer to her while I was growing up. She never graduated from college. She met and married my father and then left college to go with him. Her main thing was raising us kids. Since we left home, she doesn't seem to know what to do with herself. She wishes now she had completed college."

Brian's Feelings: "Thoughtful. I'm just like my dad. He worked and worked to get ahead. That's what I'm doing. I feel I'm going to make some terrifically bad mistakes if I'm not careful. I look at my mother, and I think, she could have done so much more. I don't want that to happen with Janet."

Janet: "My father and mother divorced when I was 15. I interviewed my mother face to face, but I had to interview my father on the phone, because he lives in another city. I think my mother's not as mad about the breakup as she used to be. She never remarried, but she's been dating someone for a year now. When my father left us, she got a job with a publisher. She has ideas all the time about books and what books the publisher should bring out next. When she gets an idea, she proposes it to the publisher. She then goes out and gets some expert to write about it. She's very successful. And she loves it. She's like Brian; she would work all the time if she could.

"My father is an engineer and works with one of the Bells. He has always liked the research work he does, and has published several articles. He remarried a few years ago, and they have two children. He seems to have more to do with that family than he ever did with ours. He seems more relaxed than I remember him when I was growing up—not so removed."

Janet's Feelings: "Hopeful. I can see in personality and abilities that I'm a lot like my father. I love it that my mother was able to find a job that she liked so much. I also love it that my father has found a happier family life. It gives me hope that I could find that for myself."

Elizabeth

"My father just retired in the last six months. It hasn't been a great adjustment. He was the king of the hill in his company. He worked for an automobile manufacturing company for almost 40 years and retired as a vice president. Since retiring, he doesn't seem to know what to do with himself. He was the classic executive workaholic. He would do anything for the company, and they rewarded him handsomely. We had to move around the country a good deal because of his job, so most of his friends were business associates. Since retiring, he's gotten more angry—almost bitter.

"My mother just managed the household. About 20 years ago, she got into a lot of volunteer work. She has now worked for years on the executive board of Planned Parenthood, and travels all over the country giving speeches and talking to political types. She's totally committed to this work. I asked her why she suddenly started doing that. Her answer was interesting: 'I had to do something. I knew your father would never change, and with you kids gone, I needed something else to be interested in. I was lucky that I had the financial security to do whatever I wanted to. I am committed to the organization and helping young women have more chances in life. It's very fulfilling.'"

Feelings: "I have always identified with my father. But I can see that, as much as I love my father, I really admire the way my mother has made a life for herself. They seem like a good business partnership. I would probably like more feeling in my relationship with my husband than they seem to have in theirs. More fun, too."

Carl

"My father died two and a half years ago. My mother is still alive and lives in an assisted living complex. I've never seen anyone so delighted to do anything as she was to tell me her life story. It's like she had been waiting years for me to ask. My father was a fairly well-known Episcopalian minister. My mother said that the first time she saw him, she knew they would get married. She played the rather demanding role of minister's wife about as well as anyone could. She never made me or my brothers do anything just to make my father look good. I always appreciated that. She insisted, sometimes over my father's strong objections, that we be allowed to think for ourselves. When he retired five years ago, he had been depressed off and on for years. He drank too much, too. He and my mother remained together through all of that. I think there was always a good deal of mutual appreciation and respect. My mother always had a wide circle of friends and when my father died, it was really nice for her to have them. A group of them moved into the same complex a few years ago. My brothers and I have remained close to her and close to each other.

"A major change happened in my mother's 'career' when she was 41. She said that, up until then, she had tried to be perfect. Lead all the church women's groups, host teas, entertain my father's guests. At this point, though, she decided that she needed to have a life of her own. She took classes at a community college, took up gardening in a big way, and started teaching in the local high school to add to the family's income. She was different after this. More sure of herself, I guess.

"I interviewed my father's younger sister. She told me an interesting story about their father, my grandfather, whom I barely knew. He worked for the railroad his entire life. He was a die-maker in the huge shops where they built locomotives and railroad cars. He started there when he was 15 and ended as a supervisor. She told me that he was highly respected among the men. His integrity and honesty were above question. He never made the first political speech, but he always represented the men in the shop to the Union. The dies he made were the patterns that they made tools from. His tools were considered some of the very best because they were so elegantly and precisely made. His sister gave me one of my grandfather's tools she had been keeping. It's very precious to me. The spirit that made him make those tools so much better than they had to be, *that* is what I feel was passed on to my father, and now to me."

"When my mother told me about her change at 41, I started thinking about myself at 41 or 42. That's when I was recruited by a headhunter to be a vice president in the entertainment company. It was quite a ride. My whole career changed like I shifted into another gear.

"I feel I am a lot like my father. If I got depressed, I could see myself drinking too much like he did. I take care of my health better than he did; I would like to live longer and be healthier."

Feelings: "Moved. Impressed with my mother's and my father's lives. Proud of what I 'inherited' from both."

NEXT CHAPTER: When you have finished your family-of-origin interviews, you are ready for integration. Your unconscious mind has been working on integrating since you began reading this book and working with the Thought Experiments. Now it is time to bring your creative unconscious work to light and use it to create a Personal Vision. Each element of Personal Vision is important. Each element is also individually complex. To pull them together into a coherent focus that can direct your career is a mammoth task. But your creative mind can do it, if you access it. The next chapter deals with the creative process and how to make purposeful use of it in forming a Personal Vision.

CHAPTER 8

Creating a
PERSONAL VISION

TO BE EFFECTIVE, A PERSONAL VISION SHOULD COM-
bine all the elements we have been discussing: stage of development, abilities, skills, personality, interests, values, goals and family of origin. Your creative mind can perform this kind of integration. Your logical mind cannot. To make creativity work,
however, you still need your logical left brain. In this chapter, we
describe the creative integration process we developed for our
clients. We call this process *left-right-left*. It uses both sides of
your brain, the logical *and* the creative, to help you achieve useful creative insights and also to make them work in the real
world.

We will show you how creative integration combines *all*
of the critical factors of career decisions into a Personal
Vision, providing an example of an actual Personal Vision
that a person has used for years to guide and enliven his
career. You can use the Thought Experiment at the end of
the chapter to start your own left-right-left integrative
process.

CREATIVITY—WHERE DOES IT COME FROM?

Many people think of creativity as a mysterious gift that some have and most don't. Many associate creativity only with purely artistic pursuits. In reality we all have creative minds and access to enormous creative talent. We just have to know how to use it.

If you boil down creativity to its pure essence, what remains is simple: a creative insight puts ideas together that no one had thought to put together before. Edison used lamp-black for a filament in an incandescent light bulb. Pasteur realized that invisible microbes in milk cause it to sour. Marie Curie realized that radiation was not a chemical reaction, but intrinsic to the element itself. Wilbur Wright suddenly understood that controlling a vehicle in the air, in three dimensions, requires a completely different system than controlling a vehicle on the ground, in two dimensions. Rachel Carson realized that the poisons we spray to kill weeds and insects eventually kill everything else. The utter obviousness of truly creative ideas often stuns us—*after* somebody thinks of them.

Think about artistic endeavors—painting a landscape, carving a sculpture, or writing a poem. Each of these creative works involves a creative insight, that is, a vision of what the painting should look like, or what the sculpture will be. That sudden connection between previously separated ideas springs from the right brain.

How do you teach your mind to think creatively? How do you learn to join two unrelated ideas to form a neat, easy solution to an "insoluble" problem? Actually, you don't have to teach your mind to do this at all. Your right brain thinks like this all the time. You just have to put it to work on the problem you want to solve.

Your right brain naturally thinks *holistically*. It solves problems by latching on to what it needs—what you remember, what you see, what you hear, what you think. The right brain does not know or care about time, and it doesn't have a strong fix on reality, either. Past, present, future, real, imagined, impossible, good, bad, profitable, impractical—they are all the same to your right brain. It doesn't make distinctions like these.

If you think about dreams you've had, you'll have a sense of how the right brain works. Your nighttime dreams don't make any logical sense. They are a mish-mash of seemingly unrelated images, feelings and events. Some dream images seem taken from life. They feel so real that you wake up and think they actually happened. Some seem to have no connection with reality at all. We know now that dreaming is our right brain's way of solving problems from day-to-day life. Psychoanalysis bases its treatment on understanding dreams and using them to make unconscious, insoluble problems both conscious and solvable.

Each of the seemingly unrelated images and events in a dream holds a complex meaning. The deeper you go into a dream the more profound and multifaceted its meaning. You can have a simple dream about a trip in a car, but the car can represent many layers of meaning. It can be, at one and the same time, simply a car, a symbol for power and control, a representation of your father and an image of yourself. Each time we dream (and experts believe that most of us dream every night whether we remember the dream or not), we create worlds and visions as complex and enlightening as the *Mona Lisa* or *Hamlet*. At night, we are all Michelangelos, Emily Dickinsons, and Mozarts.

Where is all that creativity? Why don't we feel it when we are awake? Our waking minds live in the left brain, not the right. The left brain works through words. It operates something like a digital computer. It lines up facts like parts on an assembly line and puts them together to end in a logical solution. The left brain lives in the *present*; it remembers the *past*; it thinks about the *future*. It makes clear distinctions between real and not-real, possible and impossible, profit and loss, practical and unrealistic. The left brain can plan; it can learn new facts; and it can figure out logical solutions. It's the home of the *ego*, our adult selves. It is the author of civilizations. If you think about the words on this page—lined up in logical order to express a particular meaning and no other—you have the left brain.

In contrast, look at how words are used in a poem by e.e. cummings:

> *Thy fingers make early flowers of*
> *all things.*
> *Thy hair mostly the hours love:*
> *a smoothness which*
> *sings, saying*
> *(though love be a day)*
> *do not fear, we will go amaying.*

Here you see words used by the right brain. The logic is slippery and the meaning could go down any number of paths. It's not like a digital computer. It's like the colorful images of Georgia O'Keefe, or the dark symbolism of Picasso's *Guernica*, or the baffling melting watches and clocks of Salvidor Dali. It's playful, subtle, complex, hidden and perhaps a little dangerous. It's creative.

The creative process does not happen just in the right brain. The left brain is the unsung hero. While undoubtedly creativity springs from the right brain, we don't think of people who live *just* in the right brain as creative at all. We think of them as schizophrenic—people who cannot tell the difference between reality and fantasy.

Most people who consult on creativity concentrate on helping people achieve a creative insight. But the power of creativity comes only through attention to three distinct steps involving both sides of the brain. Leave one step out and the whole process fails.

The sequence to any creative work, no matter how large or small, is always the same: *preparation, creative insight, execu-*

tion. Left-right-left. The left brain prepares the problem for the right. The right brain has the creative insight. The left brain must then translate that insight into the reality of life. What could Leonardo have done if he had not painstakingly taught himself to draw? Or if he had not taken infinite labor to learn of the engineering of his day? His insights and visions would have borne no relation to reality. They would have been the ravings of a madman. Or what would we know of Tolstoy if he had not written draft after draft of *War and Peace*? Nothing. Edison's dictum that invention is one percent inspiration and 99 percent perspiration captures the whole truth.

In *The Mustard Seed Garden*, a traditional Chinese text that teaches drawing with pen and ink, one section deals with the creative process. "First, however, you must work hard. Bury the brush again and again in the ink and grind the inkstone to dust. Take 10 days to paint a stream and five to paint a rock. If you aim to dispense with method, learn method. If you aim at facility, work hard. If you aim for simplicity, master complexity. If you wish to draw bamboo, draw bamboo every day for 10 years. Then forget about bamboo entirely. When one day you feel inspired to draw bamboo again, its pure essence emerges from the end of your brush." Left-right-left.

The left brain prepares you; it sets up the problem for you. The right brain comes up with the creative insight. The left brain must execute the insight. We consciously use this left-right-left process to help people solve one of the most complex and intricate problems imaginable, creating a Personal Vision for their careers.

CREATING A PERSONAL VISION—PREPARATION

Your left brain, even though it can't come up with the creative insight, can set up the problem. It can help you prepare. Each of the previous chapters of this book has set up a different part of the problem. Each of the Thought Experiments was part of the preparation, helping you identify and articulate a parameter of

CREATING A PERSONAL VISION

PREPARATION

ABILITIES

PERSONALITY

VALUES

SKILLS

STAGE OF DEVELOPMENT

INTERESTS

GOALS

FAMILY OF ORIGIN

Right Hemisphere Integration

INSPIRATION

A PERSONAL VISION

CREATING A PERSONAL VISION OF YOURSELF IN A MEANINGFUL FUTURE.

the problem. Even though you might not know exactly what your Personal Vision may look like, you can begin to *describe* it. For instance, "I want to be sure the fact that I am a specialist and an introvert is a positive help to me and that I don't get into a position in which I'm working against myself. That would mean I would be working in an environment in which I can spend a lot of time concentrating on one kind of task that really grabs my interest and attention."

Each time you do one of the Thought Experiments, the information is there for your left brain to use in your daily life. But it is also there for your right brain to fold into its creative musings. Doing the Thought Experiments puts your *unconscious* mind—your right brain—to work on the problem.

In our seminars, participants spend four to five weeks preparing. They learn about each of the factors we have covered—abilities, skills, interests, personality, values, goals, stage of development and family of origin. As we add information and factors, the problem of integration becomes more and more difficult. Participants begin to wonder where the process is all leading, or if they will ever be able to put everything together. For most people, some kind of inspiration strikes midway through the process. Each creative exercise produces more "ahas!" and participants start to see a path ahead. They have the beginnings of their Personal Visions.

As we noted at the end of Chapter Five, some anxiety is not only normal, it can be an important part of the creative process. Your right, unconscious brain produces anxiety as it starts to engage the problem. As a general rule, creativity happens where you are most *involved*. We are talking about *your life* and how you want that life to be. It's worth getting involved.

CREATING A PERSONAL VISION—INSPIRATION

The problem of creativity is very much the same as the problem of falling asleep. You can't make yourself fall asleep. The harder you try, the more awake you become. You can't force it, but you can set up the conditions in which it can more easily occur. You can't *make* it happen, but you can *let* it happen.

Once you set up the problem and complete your preparation, you are ready to let your right brain work on it. When you try to make creativity happen, you are using your left brain—the very brain you want to turn off so that the right brain can work. To get to your right brain, we use a three-pronged approach:

- Create an *environment* in which creativity can happen.
- Put your left brain to sleep.
- Present a problem ideally suited for the right brain, but difficult for the left.

CREATING THE RIGHT ENVIRONMENT

Setting up an environment for creativity is just as important as setting up a problem. For a creative environment, you must let go of your left brain's control for a while. You need to promise your left brain that if it will let the right brain work on the problem, it will eventually get the problem back.

How do you let go with your left brain? One way is by letting go of *results*—temporarily. Demanding that an answer be perfect and must solve all problems *now* won't gain you any creative insight, because your left brain isn't letting go of the problem. Remember, your left brain thinks in terms of the right answer, the correct solution, perfect results, even the bottom line itself—terms that make no sense whatsoever to the right brain. Your right brain can discover a new way to put the elements of your life and career together, a way that solves several different problems simultaneously. But it will take your left brain to make this insight work in your actual life. If you let the right brain work on the creative insight, trusting that your left brain has the talent and ability to translate that insight to the real world, you will have moved a long way towards creating the internal environment you will need to enhance creativity.

PUTTING THE LEFT BRAIN TO SLEEP

What is the experience of shutting down the left brain and working with the right? Most of us know this feeling, even if we don't recognize it as such. In the 1960s, some psychologists were fond of inducing an "alpha" state. A person in the alpha state felt more relaxed, lost track of time, often experienced images and sometimes insights. Today meditation is more fashionable as a term, but the state is the same—working with the right brain. In these states, we do not experience conscious thought; the logical left brain does not speak to us in words. Rather, the right brain produces dream-like images, with some words perhaps thrown in, but not in the logical manner of the left brain.

Albert Einstein once remarked that he had to be very careful not to cut himself while shaving in the morning. Not because he was clumsy, but because an idea often ignited his imagination while he was in the middle of that routine, daily chore. Ideas came to him so suddenly and forcefully that they startled him.

When we lapse into a reverie, when our minds are drifting without apparent purpose, we are using our right brains. Our left brains are asleep. We often experience this kind of reverie when listening to soothing music, or watching the movement of water, or enjoying a peaceful walk in a park.

To see how to put your left brain to sleep on purpose, let's look at meditation. People who regularly practice meditation every day carefully set it up. They use a certain room at a certain time of day. They sit in a prescribed position and breathe in and out in a prescribed way. They may say a mantra over and over to themselves. Notice the similarity to the routine and preparation for falling asleep. A certain room, a certain time, a certain preparation (change clothes, brush teeth, put out the cat), a book to read instead of a mantra. In these cases, we simply *bore* the left brain until it gives up and goes to sleep.

In the Thought Experiment at the end of this chapter, you will see that the first part of it puts your left brain to sleep. In the second part, the fun begins.

GIVING THE RIGHT BRAIN A TASK AT WHICH IT CAN EXCEL

There are some tasks that are difficult for the left brain, and quite easy for the right. Driving an automobile would be impossible if you tried to do it logically. But your right brain enjoys this kind of spatial, multifaceted task and does it easily.

As you access your right brain's creative power, you seek an *initial creative insight*, not the final answer. Your right, creative brain can only make the initial connection. Your left, logical brain makes an idea real and practical.

A young engineer had been struggling to design a truck that could be driven through rugged country to search for oil in some of the barren wastes of the West. So many different needs conflicted with so many different functions that, after six months working on the project, he was hardly further along than when he had started. His boss demanded that he present the results of his work in just two weeks, but the engineer knew he had nothing to show. In despair, he sought the help of a psychologist. After listening for an hour, the psychologist told him to come back next week and present the *worst* possible truck he could design for the purpose, a truck that would be impossible to use. The engineer feared he was wasting his time and money, but seeing no alternatives, he complied. He returned at the next session with drawings and sketches of the most outlandish contraption imaginable. He laughed so much while drawing the sketches that his wife feared the worst.

The engineer had almost not returned for that second session. There was no need. He was now working furiously on the sketches for the real presentation. While in the middle of creating the horrendous design, an insight leapt, full-blown, into his mind. "I suddenly knew where everything should go. I immediately started drawing the real designs. It was as though there were a photograph in my head and I just took the design from the photograph." The oil exploration trucks he designed are still in constant use today in Texas and Oklahoma.

The psychologist gave the engineer a task that bypassed the left hemisphere. It wasn't logical. In fact, the only way to do it was to heave logic out the window. But in doing the illogical task, the engineer's right brain gained the crucial insight into the organization of the many pieces of the engineering puzzle.

So which tasks use the right brain and bypass the left? There are an infinite variety, but we have discovered several types that are particularly successful in helping people create a Personal Vision. These tasks make use of the right brain's ability to break with hard reality and think "as if." The right brain can play with ideas and thoughts; it doesn't require logic or practicality. That's why it can come up with such creative associations.

Does this mean that whatever association the right brain develops will be valuable? Almost any strong image your right brain creates probably has some meaning for you. Messages from your right brain are never random. The complexities of your life profoundly determine each detail. They may be exceedingly difficult to translate, however. Think about the difficulty of unraveling a dream. Your left brain must translate the message.

An accountant did an exercise in which, after relaxing and allowing himself to follow a guided imagery passage, he described an ideal day. This exercise occurred after he had done a great deal of work on identifying and articulating the pieces of his Personal Vision. That is, he had already set up the problem. His image of his ideal day, as delivered by his right brain, was of himself as a circus clown: funny outfit, greasepaint, big shoes, bulbous nose—making people laugh.

Did this mean he should leave his job and join the circus? No. He lived near a circus training site, and so the sheer repetitive experience of seeing circus performers may have planted an image for his right brain to use. The accountant understood the message immediately. For many years he had been fascinated by storytelling. His grandfather had told traditional tall tales that delighted him as a child. He took every opportunity to seek out a particularly good storyteller and to listen and record the stories. A strong introvert, the accountant had never thought about what he could do with his interest. It just never occurred to him to think of it as anything but a meaningless pastime.

In looking at his natural abilities, however, he discovered that he fit a performer's profile. His personality and thinking style came together in a way characteristic of people who perform in front of others—teachers, presenters, marketing representatives, trainers and actors.

In his image of the clown, he realized that he enjoyed making people laugh and enjoyed molding his material in response to his audience. He also realized that the clown hides behind his face paint. The clown is a little removed; he is not *interacting* with the audience, but *performing*. The accountant realized he could hide, a little, behind his stories. And that he would enjoy telling them.

He is actually a gifted performer. He has not stopped being an accountant, but he has *added* something new, exciting and meaningful to his life.

A PERSONAL VISION

At age 42, the Mid-Life Turning Point, Edward, a consultant in human resources, went through the process we describe in this book. He examined all the factors—abilities, interests, skills, personality, values, goals, stage of development, family of origin—and finally went through a series of integrative exercises. This is how he describes his Personal Vision.

"My Vision came in stages. The first insights came when I got feedback on the ability battery. This was extremely enlightening—even for someone such as myself who had been through virtually every kind of development program as a part of my job. I realized that my role at work really capitalized on my natural abilities. I felt much more confident, even though I have always been successful at what I tried. It said what I had always *felt* to be true, but there it was in black and white.

"As useful as knowing about my abilities was, this did not help me make the leap to a Personal Vision. It helped fill in a few pieces, though. More pieces followed: interests, skills, personality. I started noticing a pattern. The same ideas kept emerging. When we did an integrative exercise, my Personal Vision started to take on a definite shape.

"Until that point, most of my thoughts were concerned with the structure of my job. The integrating exercises helped me broaden that perspective. In creating a Personal Vision I became more concerned with my role at work, but, just as important, *what my life would look like* as I lived out my career.

"I realized that I would need to hold several aspects of my life in balance. From my family of origin and my subsequent values, I knew my family must take an overwhelming priority. If this sounds obvious, it was not always so with me. There were times as a young professional when my family took a back seat. It was only when I consciously thought about values and priorities that I realized the personal importance of time and commitment to my family.

"My interests and talents led me toward art, which surprised me. I had never realized how important this had become to me. I suddenly "remembered" that my mother had been an artist. Also, I had never thought of myself as having anything to do with design or visual representation. But I uncovered a talent for creative design and words that has been helpful in my job and satisfying to myself. I realized I wanted to take a few more risks at work—I could be more creative in consulting with clients.

"I knew from my experience and abilities that I could create the role I wanted at work. I also knew without any doubt or hesitation that there were some roles I could be asked to fulfill that I did not have the experience, the personality, or the inclination to carry out. I knew people who could, and who would love to do it, but it wouldn't be me. This was a great insight, because I had always felt it necessary to be able to do everything. Realizing there were some roles that fit me well and other roles that didn't was enormously freeing.

"All of these elements came together in a picture I drew of my future career. I drew myself both creating and using a new technology while doing something beneficial to the world. My family was with me, and part of my attention went to them. Off to one side, I was painting, and there were sculptures that I created. As simplistic as this picture sounds when rendered in words, its *meaning* has guided most of my decisions since the day I made it."

THOUGHT EXPERIMENT G:
Creative Integration

We especially adapted this series of integrating exercises from similar ones that we do in the course of our programs. Carefully following the instructions will help you access your right, creative brain—not an easy task to do alone or on purpose.

STEP 1: PUT YOUR LEFT BRAIN TO SLEEP

Find a tape recorder you can use to record the following text. You can record it in your own voice, or you can have a spouse or friend record it for you. This will form the lead-in to all of the subsequent integration exercises. Remember that your task is to put your left brain to sleep temporarily. Your verbal left brain can relax and let go of its role in speaking to you and guiding your actions for a short time in order to let your right brain engage a problem for which it is sublimely suited.

Record the following in a slow, relaxed, well-modulated voice. Leave some pauses in your reading to give yourself a chance to picture and experience the images. We will put a note like this: [pause] where you should especially pause for a second or two. Don't worry about following the script word for word; the important thing is to relax.

RELAXATION SETUP

I want you to take a deep breath and let it out. Now take another, in and out. And as you let that one out, be aware of all of your muscles relaxing and letting go for a few minutes. All of your muscles usually have to have a certain amount of tension in them to hold you upright and help you walk around. But now they can relax for a little while and let go of their usual roles. Let your arms relax. Let your torso relax. Let your hips and legs relax. Let your neck and face relax. Let yourself drift for a little while. Let yourself drift for a moment and just enjoy this feeling of being relaxed. [pause]

Now think about a place—it can be imaginary or it can be a real place—where you feel utterly safe and secure. In your mind, get a picture of that place. [pause] Now think of yourself there, alone. What do you hear? [pause] What do you see around you? [pause] What do you smell? [pause] What are the sensations you have on your face and arms? [pause] Your back and legs? [pause] Just relax for a few minutes and enjoy the amazingly calm feeling of being in this place and enjoying all of your sensations. [pause]

You can use this tape whenever you want to work on integration. Just play it for yourself, listen to your own voice, and follow its simple instructions. This can help your left brain let go for a few minutes and let your right brain work on an exercise designed to help it make connections that would be difficult for your left brain.

This tape-recorded relaxation will be the setup for the integration exercises that come next. After the end of the relaxation sequence, wait just a few seconds, and then record the instructions you are given for the exercise you want to do.

After you do any of the exercises, *write* what you unearth in your notebook, *tell* someone else what you discovered, and/or *say* what you found out into a tape recorder. Don't worry if you don't know what an image means right now. Just describe it in words. You might have to do several integrative exercises before you "understand" the message your right brain is trying to communicate.

Make this effort to describe your image in words in order to bring your left brain back into the picture. Remember that the whole process of creative integration is *left-right-left.* You have done the preparation in the previous Thought Experiments. These exercises help your right brain integrate, but to *claim* your right-brain discoveries, you must translate them to your left brain.

STEP 2: CREATIVE INTEGRATION

We suggest you read the following exercises and decide which one most strikes your imagination. The more you can approach any of the exercises with a feeling of "Let's just see what happens," the more open you can be to whatever your right brain may have to give you. Don't worry if you can't see the sense in an image or thought right now. Trust your left brain to decipher it later. In the next chapter on Surveying, you will learn how to make your vision work in a practical sense in the real world. For now, you can just let your right brain play with the pieces of the puzzle without getting too uptight about its final form.

GUIDED IMAGERY
Record the following after your relaxation setup:

Now, in your imagination, I want you to get up gradually and look around. Again, sense how safe, secure, and comfortable you are feeling. Notice a path leading away from where you are. You don't exactly know where this path leads, but you feel it would definitely be worth your while to find out. You decide to take this path. It winds through some territory that is familiar to you, and some that is new. You have a pleasant sensation of moving, feeling your legs step confidently one after the other and feeling your footsteps plant solidly and strongly one after another on the path. You hear the leaves around you stirred by a cool breeze and feel the pleasant and cool air on your cheek. You still feel totally safe and secure. Your feeling is that of exploring a new and fascinating territory and making interesting discoveries.

Finally you come to a large body of water. It is calm, but you can't see the other side. There is a boat nearby. It is exactly suited for the purpose of carrying you safely to the other side. You get in and push off. You guide the boat yourself. You feel entirely in control of it.

Soon you see the shore. Gradually it comes more clearly into view. Finally you feel the prow of the boat crunch gently into the sand. You step out and realize that you are in a different place. It is a place where you always wanted to be, even if you never quite realized it before. You look around and realize that this is the place where you will be living your life sometime in the future. It is your fullest, most satisfying, and most complete life. All of the important elements are here, and all of the important things you want to do are ready for you to take up and do. All of the important people that need to be here are here.

What is around you? [pause]

Where do you live? [pause]

Where do you work? [pause]

What is the main feeling of your life? [pause]

Who is here in this place with you? [pause]

What do you do with your days? [pause]

What is a typical day like? [pause]

What is the most important thing you do in a day? [pause]

What is next? [pause]

What are your most important relationships? [pause]

What is the role you play in your relationships? [pause]

Just enjoy this life for a few minutes, and when you are ready, wake up and write in your notebook everything about your image you can remember, no matter how unimportant it may seem. Include your answers to the questions asked. If you want, you can also tell someone important to you about your image, or record it on tape. Again, try to describe the image in detail, even if the meaning is not clear to you right now.

TAKING AWAY AN IMPEDIMENT

Record the following instructions after your relaxation setup:

Many people seem to live life habitually as though they were *forced* to do everything they do. "I have to go to work to earn money to support my children and spouse. I have to put up with work I don't find particularly meaningful because if I didn't, I wouldn't have a job. My boss is abusive but if I don't endure it,

I'll be fired."

We find that people have far more choice in life than they usually think they do. They live life as though forced to endure it, but when they decide what they want, and go after it, they often succeed.

We designed exercises like this to give you the sense of choice. If you could choose to do anything, what would you do? [pause]

Imagine that you woke up one morning and found that the life you thought you had been living was actually a dream. Your actual life, the one to which you just woke up and now realize is the real one, is almost exactly like the one you had dreamed, except for one key difference. You realize you have a bank account that you can draw on any time you want and this bank account has many millions of dollars in it. You realize that you never have to worry about earning money again. You have all the money you can possibly ever need or that anyone close to you could possibly need. You could start each day asking yourself, "O.K., what do I want to do today?" And then do whatever came to you.

What would your life be like? [pause]

How would you spend your time? [pause]

What would your relationship with your spouse or partner be like? [pause]

What about your children? [pause]

How about with your parents? [pause]

Who would be your friends? [pause]

What would you talk to them about? [pause]

How would you feel about your days? [pause]

How would you feel about your life? [pause]

Now describe a typical day as you would live it. What would you do? [pause]

Where would you go? [pause]

What would give your life meaning? [pause]

What would be the most important thing you would do with your life? [pause]

Now open your eyes and write down all that you can remember of your images and the answers to the questions in your notebook. Write down anything else that seems important from your image. Remember that it doesn't have to make any sense right now. Any message your right brain comes up with may be something your left brain will be able to use. Again, if you prefer, you can tell someone important, or record it on tape.

LOOKING BACKWARDS

Record the following instructions after your relaxation setup:

Now I want you to imagine that you are much older and have lived a very long and productive life. You are still quite healthy and active. You have accomplished the many things you set out to do with your life, not only in your career, but also in your family life and in your personal life. You feel content and satisfied. Your life has been remarkably full and interesting.

A teacher in a local junior high school has given her pupils an assignment: interview an older person about his or her life and find out what advice, ideas and wisdom he or she would like to pass on to a younger generation just starting out in life. One of the pupils, 12 years old, comes to interview you. Here is what the young student would like to know:

What are the most important things you have accomplished? [pause]

How have you changed over the years? [pause]

What used to be important to you that isn't so important now? [pause]

What used not to be important that feels a lot more important to you now? [pause]

What are your most important relationships? [pause]

How have you nurtured and maintained them over the years? [pause]

How have you managed to stay so healthy and vital all these

years? [pause]

How have you managed to stay so alert and interested in life? [pause]

What is the most important piece of advice you could give to someone just starting out about how to live life? [pause]

What else would you like to say about your life? [pause]

What other advice would you give to a young person? [pause]

Now open your eyes and write down all that you can remember about your answers to the questions and about your thoughts and feelings during the exercise. If you prefer, you can tell someone or record your impressions.

FOUR STORIES: INTEGRATION

Tracy

"This was fun. I did all three of the exercises and got something interesting from all of them. Science kept emerging. And the environment. Also different cultures. I could see myself investigating interesting problems about the environment and producing something that would be of significant benefit to the world. When I gave advice to the 12-year-old, I was a scientist who had made some important discoveries about the habitats around the coral reefs. I told the young boy that he should find something that was completely fascinating and pursue it like crazy. Don't worry too much about money. Worry more about doing something meaningful and that you feel passionate about."

Brian and Janet

Brian: "When I did the exercise about removing an impediment I got a rude awakening. If I had all the money I needed to live on—more than I could spend—I wouldn't have anything to do. I could almost picture myself being like my mother: directionless, flat, trying to find something to occupy her time. I did the exercise on giving advice, too. The main advice I gave was, 'Find something worth living for.' Neither my parents nor Janet's parents have had very strong marriages. Unless Janet and I do something different, we could easily drift apart, too. I could see agreeing to have a baby just to give Janet something to do, turning the entire parenting thing over to her, and then ending up just like my mother and father. I'm rethinking this whole deal. Maybe I've been missing something important."

Feelings now: "Very, very thoughtful."

Janet: "When I did the exercise on an ideal day, I had this clear image of doing a research project. I would ask people questions about what they wanted and how they liked things, and then figure out from their answers how to make them happier with our service. I could work on my own projects and think about them as much as I wanted to. The whole image makes me happy. When I described it to Brian, he said, 'Why don't you do it?' At that moment I realized that's exactly what I could do. I could do detailed research on customers so that the company would be able to avoid some complaints and pitch its services more toward what people already want. Brian said that marketing could use that kind of information. This is all tremendously exciting to me. For the first time, I felt I could do a job that was really *me*."

Feelings now: "Very excited."

Elizabeth

"When I did the exercise about my ideal day, the image I had was of working hard, solving problems, doing something interesting, quitting at 5:30, and going home to be with my children and husband. And I don't mean taking a big briefcase home with me, either. I mean really *being* with my family. It was a wonderful image. I told my husband about it, and he said, 'Sure, honey. You know you could never do that.' I started thinking, 'Why not?'

"The second image I had was when I did the exercise on looking back. The advice I gave was, 'Find something you're really passionately interested in, and make it happen.' What's interesting was that in the image of myself in this exercise, I was a famous innovator in children's day care."

Feelings now: "Excited. Energetic. I think I know what I want to do. First of all, I'm going to start working more normal hours. I will make that happen. Second, I'm going to look into day care at our company. Maybe there are a whole range of child-related services the company could offer its employees. I know of some innovative programs. I'll find out about them."

Carl

"This was easy. My ideal day was working for the Free Clinic. I enjoy it and enjoy the people there. I feel like I'm doing something for people that they really need. The feeling I get working there is exhilarating.

"When I did the 'taking away an impediment' exercise, I was still doing something like the Free Clinic. I was in charge of it. Which is interesting, because the executive director of the last 12 years is leaving in three months. They've already offered me another job on staff. I'm thinking about looking at that executive director position.

"My advice to the student was this: do something you enjoy; do something you find meaningful. Don't wait around until you're old before you realize you ought to enjoy what you do."

Feelings now: "Excited. I haven't felt this enthusiastic about anything in at least a couple of years."

NEXT CHAPTER: The ideas and images you might gain from these exercises may help you start to crystallize a vision—an image of what you want your future to look like and how you want to live in it. As you start to get an image of this future, you are ready to Survey. Surveying is a practical, reality-based, hands-on way to translate your image or picture into substantive reality and into a solid path to get you there. In the next chapter we describe Surveying. The Thought Experiment will help you carry out a Survey interview.

CHAPTER 9

Surveying to Make Your Personal VISION REAL

THE MOST DIFFICULT PART OF CREATIVITY MAY HAP-
pen *after* the creative insight. In fact, lack of attention to this
step is probably what sinks most creative ideas. You can have
the most imaginative Personal Vision of all, but it won't help
you unless you connect it to the marketplace.

Surveying is a tool we use to help bridge the gap between
integrative insight and reality. It is powerful, subtle and
remarkably effective. Let's look at how it worked with Jim, a
young manager.

SURVEYING

Jim, a production manager, had a creative idea for tightening
production schedules. His idea came to him in a dream. The
whole production process could be organized more efficiently
with little additional cost and a reduction in total manpower
needs. He couldn't wait to get to work to tell his boss.

When he launched into telling her how production should
be reorganized, he was surprised and disconcerted as his won-

derful idea melted away. What came out was only a pale shadow of his whole idea, and the more questions his boss asked, the thinner and more insubstantial it became. He finally realized that she was just listening politely and didn't get the power of the idea at all.

Jim did have a creative idea, but he had not done any work to make it real. The idea came out of his right brain; it came from a dream. To explain it to anyone else, he would have to translate it to the left hemisphere. He would have to put it into words.

People generally have the same experience as Jim when they try to put their most creative thoughts into words. What at its inception was a rich, colorful idea becomes one-dimensional, ordinary, and limited. In spite of this, it is only by translating an idea into words that we gain control of it, that we have the ability to use and exploit it.

Frustrated by his first attempt to convince his boss, Jim worked through his idea again.

First of all, he drew a picture of this plan to reorganize production. Then he wrote it down on a flow sheet. The flow sheet detailed every aspect of production affected by the changes. He practiced talking about the changes with his wife, explaining his chart point by point. He told her about the problem his changes were designed to help, and how his idea would improve overall production. His wife didn't know anything about the production process, but asked Jim questions that sent him back to his flow sheet to reorganize and solve some major problems in his proposal.

As Jim got more excited about his idea and determined to see if it would be helpful, he noticed an article in a trade magazine in which a manager talked about organizing information systems. The recommendations the manager proposed were structurally very much like those that Jim proposed.

Jim called the author of the article. They talked for several hours over four different conversations. Jim felt energized. For the first time since his original conception, he *knew* his idea would work.

With his boss's permission, Jim then went to other people in the production process who would be affected by change. He talked to a number of them, explaining to each one what he saw as a problem, and then discussed his idea. Each time he did this, he further refined his original idea. He had not taken into account some important details in his first conception. In some instances, the changes Jim proposed would create new problems.

When Jim returned to his boss, it was with a written proposal for change. He detailed not only exactly what he thought should be changed, and how, but also what he projected the results would be. He addressed the kind of real-world detail that adds richness and texture to a proposal. He also addressed potential problems and how to solve them.

At this point, to his boss, the decision was obvious. What Jim was proposing would save a great deal in time and effort, cutting out needless redundancies. Jim had thought about it from every angle and it looked quite promising.

It is important to keep in mind that the basic proposal Jim described to his boss the day after his dream was *exactly the same proposal* that his boss later thought was a no-brainer. What changed was that Jim made the creative idea real.

THE PROCESS OF MAKING AN IDEA REAL

The process Jim used to transform his original insight into an effective, compelling presentation may seem far removed from figuring out what to do in your career, but it is not. If you are to make any move in your career, you will need to convince someone else. You will need to make a compelling case for whatever you decide you want to do, whether it is to shift to a new responsibility at your present job, let go of a task that drives you crazy, change jobs altogether, go to graduate school, or jump into a field right out of college. Whatever you want to do, you will have to tell some critical people and convince them it's a good idea. Even if you realize you want to stay precisely where you are, you still have to make a compelling case to *yourself*. Otherwise you are trapped.

Surveying makes the vital connection between the reality of yourself and your dreams, and the reality of the marketplace. It helps you find your exact fit.

To begin Surveying, you must have an idea. We designed the previous Thought Experiments to bring in all of the important career factors and help you creatively integrate them and figure out a Personal Vision. Your Personal Vision can give you direction and focus, or simply someplace to start looking. Without this kind of focus, Surveying can't happen.

So let's say that you have an idea about what you are looking for, or what you would like to be doing with your life, or how you would like to be living. If your idea sprang from a strong connection to yourself, then it can form the nucleus of your Survey work.

THE STEPS OF SURVEYING

Step 1: Write it down; force yourself to put the idea, as completely as possible, in words in your notebook. Get the flow and sequence right. Put it on a time line. When do you want to be doing this? What are the intermediate steps? What will you have to do first in order to arrive where you want to be? Put those on a time line also.

Step 2: Tell someone outside your systems. It has been said that you don't really know something until you can explain it to a reasonably intelligent seven-year-old. A person outside your systems has no agenda or preconceptions about you and your career, and doesn't know anything about the issues or the problems with which you are dealing. You will find out a great deal by talking to a person like this about your plans. You can use this information to revise your original idea.

SURVEYING TO MAKE A PERSONAL VISION REAL

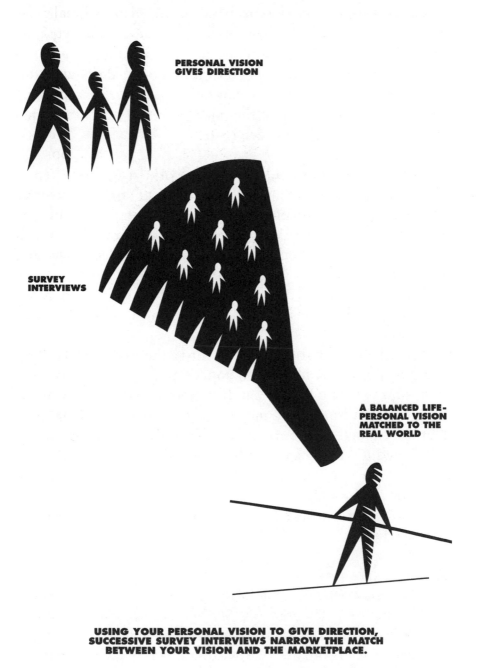

PERSONAL VISION GIVES DIRECTION

SURVEY INTERVIEWS

A BALANCED LIFE - PERSONAL VISION MATCHED TO THE REAL WORLD

USING YOUR PERSONAL VISION TO GIVE DIRECTION, SUCCESSIVE SURVEY INTERVIEWS NARROW THE MATCH BETWEEN YOUR VISION AND THE MARKETPLACE.

Step 3: This is the critical step of Surveying: *finding someone who is doing the same thing, or close to it*. Once you have a clear, verbal conception of your idea, you can find someone doing something very close to your idea. It may be in a different arena, or with a different process, but the *idea* may still be similar. Interview this person and find others to interview. The Thought Experiment at the end of this chapter deals with this Survey Interview. It can save you hours of planning and going down dead-ends. It can be the most powerful and useful step you take in making your idea real.

Step 4: After considerable Survey work, make a presentation. This should combine all of the elements of your creative conception with how you have molded and modified your idea to work in the real world. This presentation should start with what your idea has to do with you. What abilities, skills, and interests of yours does it relate to? What values and goals does it fulfill? How does your personality aid you in carrying out your idea? What does your idea relate to in your past or in your family of origin?

Then the presentation should shift to the marketplace. You must be able to tell the person you are trying to convince how your idea will help him or her. If you were making a presentation for a business, for instance, you would need to have learned enough about the marketplace through your Survey Interviews to know exactly what needs your idea will fill. You will need to know enough to overcome all of the inevitable questions.

So how does it work? Let's pick up Ruth's story from an earlier chapter.

RUTH'S STORY, CONTINUED

You may remember the story of Ruth, the buyer of Italian cloth, from Chapter Six. She didn't just stumble into a perfect job. She had done all the work of creating a Personal Vision. She had written down what she knew of it. You may remember that the idea she started with, although well connected to her abilities and other personal factors, was vague and ill-formed. She wanted to work in an artistic field. She wanted to use her skills acquired in her years as a buyer. She had a particular affinity for the artistic qualities of cloth and fiber. She wrote down everything she could to describe the position she sought, even though she did not know yet what that position was.

Ruth told her idea to people outside her systems. This is an important step, often overlooked. Ruth first proposed her idea following an integration exercise. "I had this crazy idea of working with cloth. You know, buying special cloth." She was ready to reject the idea entirely and go on to something more practical. The other people in her workshop weren't in her systems, though. *They* didn't see what was crazy about it. They saw how well it matched much of what she wanted in life. In our programs when people have really creative ideas, they frequently want to reject them at first. But people *outside* your immediate systems can often see creative solutions as genuine innovations.

Ruth determined to make her idea real. She started Survey Interviews. She started a chart to record her Survey work. Using the interview format you will find in the Thought Experiment, she interviewed people in positions suggested by her description of her ideal career. She interviewed two museum directors and several curators and museum archivists. She interviewed several creative and design people from advertising firms. She interviewed many interior designers and decorators.

Each time she interviewed someone, she found out first about that person, as an individual, then about that person's job, then about the company that person worked for, and finally about the whole field in which the person worked. (As you will see in the Survey Thought Experiment, this is a useful order for asking questions in a Survey Interview.) Although Ruth was offered three different jobs during the course of her Survey work, she always insisted from the outset of each interview that she was not looking or asking for a job, but for information. She was not ready to propose a job, because she didn't know enough.

Ruth interviewed designers and buyers for design shops. With every interview, she learned more about the tight little area of work in which she had become interested, and she found more people to interview. She filled up several posters with her Survey notes. When she understood how difficult it was for upscale design studios to find unusual art cloth, she saw that many had a problem for which she was uniquely qualified to provide an answer.

At this point, Ruth met and interviewed the architect to whom she would eventually make her proposal. Long before this, she had noticed a change in her interviews. She often knew more about what was happening in the field and in the area of interest to her than the people she interviewed. Often they asked *her* questions about what was going on, because she was so clearly knowledgeable.

In the course of her interviews, Ruth met a person who had tried to import art cloth, but could never find a ready market. Ruth was sure she had enough contacts to create and sustain a market for this cloth. She felt ready for a presentation. She saw the architect as having the most pressing need, so she decided to start there.

Ruth scheduled another interview with the architect—this would be her third. This time she told him that she wanted to make a presentation to him that would be of interest. She outlined her whole idea, starting with herself, moving to the architect's need for unusual art cloth, to how she would propose to work with him. For the architect, it was obvious. Ruth had known it would be.

Surveying, as a process, is much like a funnel, large at the top, smaller and more focused as you progress. Starting with a largely unfocused idea, Ruth was yet able to use it to begin her Survey work. In the course of almost 50 interviews over several months, she eliminated a number of dead-ends and uncovered several likely avenues. As she continued to explore, her focus narrowed. As she found out more and more about a progressively narrow field, her idea became more precise, and more attuned to marketplace demand. When she made her proposal, it was exactly suited not only to what *she* wanted to do, but also to what she knew the market needed.

SURVEYING AT TURNING POINTS

At every Turning Point we need a Personal Vision. At every Turning Point we should Survey. The better idea we have of the road ahead, the better we can make decisions about our lives.

Starting in 1990, we, the authors, both 42, both at the Mid-Life Turning Point, spent more than two years Surveying. Beginning with an idea for a new business, we interviewed anyone we could find who did anything remotely similar to what we had in mind. We personally went through any program we could find that related to the issue. We interviewed hundreds of potential competitors, potential customers, and business people in other fields entirely, but who used a business structure we might want to use. At each interview we took away invaluable information. Even if it turned out that a person did nothing remotely similar to what we had in mind, we focused our thoughts, narrowed our ideas, and became more precise and knowledgeable in presenting our case each time we talked to someone.

Our experience in helping people launch new ideas in their careers—whether they have ideas for whole new businesses or only for a slight shift in job responsibilities—is that they ignore this step too often. The more Survey work you do *before* your presentation, the stronger your case will be and the more confident and solid you will feel in your presentation.

Let's take the case of Sharon, an advertising director at a large public utility.

Sharon's Story

Sharon went through the entire process of creating a Personal Vision. What she found out startled her. She had many more abilities than her staff position made use of. She realized she was not interested in her job and that it failed to challenge her or push her to grow. She wanted her job to express more of her unique talents. (Often managers ask us what the *company* gets out of letting its employees go through a process of gaining a Personal Vision. Some feel that if employees really looked carefully at what they are expected to do, they would quit and do something else. Some feel that their employees are already highly motivated. Our overwhelming experience is that people who create a Personal Vision feel more connected to their companies *and* their careers because they learn exactly how to position and utilize their unique talents. They also feel less stressed and less burned-out for the same reasons.)

Soon after Sharon went through the program, an internal memo came across her desk: the company wanted to hire a national accounts manager. Making such a shift would be unusual, but Sharon knew she had the right mix of abilities, talents, personality, and interests for the job. Over a period of two weeks, Sharon pulled out her Personal Vision statement and used it to craft a careful description of how she saw herself carrying out the new job. She then interviewed the person who had just vacated the position, three people who were in similar positions in the company, and five people who would be reporting to her should she get it. After each interview she revised her plan and wrote down what she had learned.

Sharon applied for the job. One of the people who interviewed her was someone *she* had interviewed about it just the week before. She had become knowledgeable about the position and the system by interviewing others. She made a compelling and clear presentation of herself and her vision. She started with her interests, even as a young child, went to her natural abilities, her personality and her demonstrable skills, and continued with her strong values. She showed clearly how all these different aspects of herself interlocked and made her qualified, not just by her skills, but by her heart and talents. The case she made was airtight—a slam dunk. She is now a national accounts manager.

She would never have thought about this opportunity had she not looked carefully at her career and life to understand more fully what she wanted. Her Personal Vision was like a template. When the right job came along, she recognized it instantly. By Surveying, Sharon made her Vision real.

THOUGHT EXPERIMENT H:
Surveying Interview, Survey Presentation

Surveying is the most powerful tool we have for making creative ideas real. You can never know enough about a market or a field. Each time you do a Survey Interview, even if it seems that you didn't find out anything new, you force yourself to challenge your ideas against the reality of the marketplace. You become sharper, more focused and more realistic in what you can and cannot do.

THE SURVEY INTERVIEW

WHEN TO INTERVIEW

The Survey Interview can serve several purposes in the whole process of career self-management. At the beginning, you can use it to make your Personal Vision more focused and related to the marketplace. Starting with even a vague notion, so long as it gives you some direction, you can interview people to find out about them, their jobs and careers, and the fields they are in. Each time you do this, you will narrow your focus by making your Personal Vision more realistic.

You can continue this process of narrowing your Personal Vision almost indefinitely, making it more precise until your idea crystallizes. When you feel more certain about what you want to do, you can continue to use Surveying to gain valuable knowledge about the field and about systems. As noted in the body of the chapter, when people you interview start asking you questions because they recognize your knowledge and expertise in the area, you know you will soon be ready to make a presentation. This may take several months, as in Ruth's case, or even several years, as in the authors'.

WHOM TO INTERVIEW

Let your Personal Vision guide you. Even if it seems ill-formed and unfocused, it can give you clues about whom you should interview. At first, you can gain valuable insight from anyone who does anything even remotely like what you have in mind. As you do each interview, you will learn more and find other people to talk to. You will also become increasingly precise about *whom* you interview and *what* exactly you are trying to find out.

SETTING UP THE INTERVIEW

Setting up the interview lays the tone and groundwork for the interview itself. Paying attention to details in the setup can insure a successful outcome.

Call the person and state who you are and how you were referred. Let's say this person is a woman who manages an organization in a style similar to the way you are interested in managing. When you call, tell her that you would like to meet for 30 minutes or so at her convenience. You are not selling anything. You are not looking for a job. You are only interested in the way she manages her organization. Explain how you found out about her. Make every effort to accommodate her schedule and time.

CONDUCTING THE INTERVIEW

Start with the person herself. How did she decide to get into her present career? What were the decisions she made at Turning Points? What was her reasoning at each?

    College to Work (age 22-25)
    Age-30 Assessment (age 28-33)
    Mid-Life Transition (age 38-45)
    Age-50 Assessment (age 50-55)
    Pre-Retirement Transition (age 60-65)

    How did she move into her present position?
    What does she like about it? What does she dislike?
    How did she come to adopt her present management style?
    How would she describe it?

Describe a recent day that she felt was productive and that
she enjoyed.

What made it enjoyable?

What made it productive?

Describe a recent bad day or one that was unproductive.

What made it bad?

What made it unproductive?

What does she see for her own future?

What does she see for the future of this field (industry,
company)?

What has helped and guided her most over the years?

What advice would she have for someone just starting out?

Again, just as with the family interviews, use these questions
to give yourself a springboard for the interview. If anything
strikes your interest, pursue it. Remember, you are asking this
person, as a favor to you, to talk about the most fascinating subject on earth—herself and her opinions. You don't have to agree
with everything she says; just listen. If you approach it openly,
you will learn a great deal, even from interviews in which you
thoroughly disagree with every point your subject makes. Your
job is not to change this person's mind, but to learn something
that will be valuable to you in making your Personal Vision real.

When you have done enough Survey Interviews to be thoroughly knowledgeable about the field and what you want to
do in it; to recognize the best fit for your abilities, personality,
interests, values and goals; to understand others' needs that
your Personal Vision could contribute to; and to plan how you
want to go about implementing your Vision, you may be ready
for a presentation.

YOUR PRESENTATION

Start your presentation with yourself. Ideally, list what you
have learned about your talents, interests, personality, skills,
experience, values, goals and even family of origin and stage of

development. This is the most effective way to communicate who you are, what you have to offer, and why. Next, talk about what you know to be the needs of the organization or the person to whom you are presenting. Your Survey work will pay off here if you can speak knowledgeably and cogently. Link yourself to the company's needs by means of your Personal Vision, showing how the sum total of your personal career factors contributes to fulfilling a need in the company. (If you find you can't make this link, or that it appears weak, this may be a signal that you need to do more Surveying.)

FOUR STORIES: SURVEYING

Tracy

"I have interviewed about 10 people so far. I started with a microbiologist at the university. He was interesting, and let me tag along with him for a day to see what he did. I knew from that that I wasn't interested in pure science. I need to see some result that is closer to the real world. He pointed me in the direction of a friend of his who is a behavioral biologist. Her work is almost all theoretical. But it was interesting to talk to her about how she sees it being useful to people—eventually. After her, I interviewed a biochemist. He introduced me to some people running a primate research lab. That was more like it. I interviewed several of their research people and talked to them about their projects. I liked the whole feel of the place, and I was interested in what they are doing. After I had had two or three interviews there, and been back to spend a day with one of the researchers, one of them told me to apply to be a tech assistant there. So I did. And now that's what I'm doing, working full time. I am also planning on taking a graduate course in primate biology and evolution at the university. I am pretty sure I will go to graduate school in the next couple of years, but I feel the experience I'm getting now in hands-on research is wonderful, so I'm not in a crashing hurry. The scientists I'm working with have connections all over, and I'm sure they can help me get into a good graduate program when I'm ready. I don't think I'll spend my career in primate research, but I know I will go to graduate school in some area of biology. Lately, I have become fascinated with marine mammals."

Feelings now: "For the first time since I quit psychology, I feel like I know what I'm doing. I know I have a long way to go, but that's OK, because I have this clear image of doing something interesting and meaningful."

Brian and Janet

Brian: "My first question was, whom do I interview? I'm already doing what I like. Then, as I got to thinking about it, I realized that the real question for me was how to have a life *besides* work. My father never has. When I put it this way, I thought of a story someone had told me about an older guy in Human Resources. He had refused some assignments because it would take him away from his family. At least that was the story. I found out who the guy was, and called him up. When I said what I wanted, he immediately suggested we have lunch. It was more than interesting. He decided early in his career that he would not let his work take him from his family and that he would not ask his family to move around unreasonably. I asked him if he felt it had hurt his career. He said, in the short run, yes, though not as much as you might be afraid it would. In the long run, he's accomplished much of what he wanted to do in his career and has ended up in charge of a major portion of Human Resource services nationwide. I would like to end up like him. He gave me the names of a couple of other executives in different departments who have done the same thing. I called them and talked to both of them a long time on the phone. The more I talked to them, the more I realized that it is more possible to have a life than I thought. It's going to be rough for the next five or six years, but if I don't start making room for a family now, I could wind up divorced like about half the people I know.

"Next, I took my boss to lunch and set out the whole deal to him. I went through my abilities, interests, personality, values, goals—even what I found out about my family. After that I told him what I wanted to do and why, and asked him if he could help. He was actually very sympathetic, and quite helpful. He likes my work a lot and feels that I have real promise with the company. He said I would have to set limits on my time myself, but that he would help by making sure I got some good projects. He doesn't know what effect this will have on my being chosen for the fast track."

Brian's feelings now: "Determined. I feel I am sort of sailing into unknown territory. The company would like it if I worked 24 hours a day. To tell the truth, a part of me feels I *should* work around the clock if the company needs it. But I need a whole life, too. So does Janet. If we are going to have a family, we have to make it a priority for both of us."

Janet: "I did some research and found out there is a company in town that does market research. I called them up and got to talk to one of their senior researchers. He was very happy to talk to me when I explained what I wanted. We met and talked probably two hours about what he did. This was fascinating. It was like doing a research project for your work. He gave me the names of two other people in the field, and I interviewed both of them. One of them gave me the name of someone doing market and customer research in a large corporation. This would be more like my own situation, so I was eager to interview her. She helped, because, as it turned out, she had started her own little unit of customer research in this company about 10 years ago.

She had been able to show tremendous benefit to the company over that time for very little outlay. This would give me a strong case to my bosses. She offered me a job there, but by this time, I was already feeling I could get my own show going in my company. Over the next three months, I continued interviewing. I also started some preliminary talks with some people in my company about what I had in mind and why. I wanted to get an idea about what roadblocks I would probably run into. I finally wrote up a proposal in which I showed what other companies' experiences had been with ongoing formal customer/market research. I made a formal pitch and they are going to let me proceed on a trial basis. This whole project is the most exciting thing I have ever done."

Janet's feelings now: "Tremendously happy and proud of what I've accomplished. Brian and I are planning to have a baby after next year. I want to get this project rolling. I am finding out something new every day and I couldn't be happier."

Elizabeth

"The first thing I did was go to my boss and tell him that I was out of here at 5:30. I was not going to travel, and I wouldn't work at night. That was rash, I know, and I was holding my breath after I said it. He looked at me and said, 'OK.' I didn't know whether I'd be able to stick to it or not, but mostly I have. I've had to travel some, but I have also been able to turn down some travel. I do leave between 5:30 and 6:00 every day. My family responded immediately. Things have been much less stressed at home. I have had to force myself to be more organized and to be clearer about my priorities. I also delegate better. I think I am actually working so much more effectively that I get everything that absolutely needs to be done accomplished.

"The second thing I have been working on is company-sponsored day care. I've probably interviewed 50 people, from day-care operators to consultants to human-resource people to architects. This has been interesting. I know we'll win eventually. I have my own team of people from all over the company who are now working on this project—all on our own time. The company hasn't quite understood the idea yet, nor do they see the benefits. Other companies are sponsoring day care for employees' children, and we will have to solve a number of significant problems to bring it off, but I am sure we are right. Anyway, the whole project is very exciting."

Feelings now: "Excited. Creative. Alive."

Carl

"I went right away and interviewed the executive director of the Free Clinic. It is very intriguing. Resources are quite limited, and a large part of the role is fund-raising and public relations. I have a lot of contacts in the business community, and I think I could build some corporate sponsorships. The only thing holding me back is the pay. It would be a lot less than I had been making. On the other hand, my wife and I are pretty well set as far as retirement and college for the kids is nearly over, so I think we could make do with less. I am pretty sure from talking to the Board members of the Free Clinic that I would have a good shot at the position, and I think I will ask them to consider me for it.

"I feel I could always go back into business somewhere, but I realize I would be disappointed to do so. The opportunity to work at the Free Clinic is much more exciting to me, even if it won't pay as well."

Feelings now: "Happy."

NEXT CHAPTER: The next chapter shows how people have used their Personal Visions at different career Turning Points to make their lives and careers more satisfying and productive, and to set themselves up to grow into future Turning Points.

CHAPTER 10

Your Personal Vision As Guide for Your LIFE AND CAREER

YOUR PERSONAL VISION IS A WAY TO SEE INTO THE future. More important, it links you to that future. It points the way, it works as a template for making decisions, and it draws you forward. One of the primary characteristics of happy, productive, successful people is that they *see themselves in a future that feels positive and attainable*.

The opposite is also true. A defining characteristic of people experiencing stress, anger, depression, boredom, ennui and burnout is that they do *not* see themselves in a future that feels positive. They don't like the way things are going, and they don't see it changing. They are caught in the Stress Cycle.

When people don't have Personal Visions they confuse their systems' goals and interests with their own goals and interests. The goals they seek are actually their systems' goals. They move toward a future that is not really their own, but their systems'.

SOME THOUGHTS ABOUT PERSONAL VISION

The more objectively connected your Personal Vision is to

yourself, the better it can guide your career. Your Personal Vision must come from *inside* to be effective; no one can hand it to you. If you don't follow a *structure* to create your Personal Vision, you run the risk of leaving out key aspects of your life that may prove critically important later. You also run the risk of viewing yourself and your options through the distorting lens of your systems. The more solidly and objectively your Personal Vision grounds you in your present life, the more surely it moves you into the future.

No matter how accurate the Personal Vision you create now, change will occur. Our lives all move in regular cycles from Turning Point to periods of stability to Turning Point. No matter how satisfied we have been with a career, there are times when we long for change. No matter how dissatisfied and unhappy we are during periods of stability, we continue along the same path without changing—until we arrive at another Turning Point.

Work you do to create a complete and viable Personal Vision not only helps you at the present Turning Point; it also continues to help you at future Turning Points. Opening options at one Turning Point can give you more options at the next, just as shutting down options at a Turning Point can easily limit your options later.

As we move through our lives and careers, each Turning Point builds on the strengths and weaknesses of the process we used at the last one. Knowledge about your abilities, skills, interests, personality, values, goals and family of origin, as well as ideas and answers for putting them together, help you every time you face a decision. If you make career choices enlightened by a clear Personal Vision, these decisions can help you grow and experience your life more fully. When you get to the next Turning Point, you not only have a useful structure for figuring that one out, you also have several years of fuller, more successful, more enthusiastic experience under your belt from which to draw.

If, when faced with change, you ignore increasingly negative feelings, you can certainly survive Turning Points intact. But you will not have found out any more about yourself. You will have missed one of the most powerful opportunities in life to figure out who you really are and what you really want.

The same can be said of unconsidered, radical or catastrophic change at Turning Points. This ostensibly sudden change only occurs after years of unrecognized and unexpressed unhappiness. The results of catastrophic change usually mirror closely results of doing nothing at Turning Points. Great sweeping changes throw away many advantages of long experience. Starting over from scratch means that you spend your time and creative energy getting back to the point at which you started, rather than exploring new territory. No real learning takes place. And an opportunity to figure out what could really feel productive and satisfying and create more meaning in your life goes to waste.

When people limit their options at Turning Points, it becomes more and more difficult to open new options later in life. Not because options aren't available, but because it becomes increasingly difficult to see anything outside of the Stress Cycle.

CREATING THE BALANCE CYCLE

The nature of humans and systems is such that balance doesn't just happen. We have to create it consciously. We learn how to fashion our lives from our parents. Obviously, if our parents live stressfully, we learn to live stressfully, too. Any life outside the Stress Cycle would seem unnatural.

But what about parents who *do* balance work and family, productivity and connectedness—parents who grow and change throughout their lives, adapting effectively to changes in their environments and in themselves? This example is incalculably valuable for the child who is to become an adult. Parents like this have held steadfastly to an *interior* sense of themselves and what they want, and consistently held this interior sense of self as more important than the self their systems see.

The children of these parents learn to create an interior sense of self, too. They also learn that this interior sense is more important than the self the system sees. But these children will need to be just as active in creating and retaining a Personal Vision as their parents were. They will have to move purposefully into the Balance Cycle.

Children in such families learn that they are not one person now and forever. Rather, our True Selves constantly learn, grow, and change. Our systems, including our schools, colleges, corporations, and families, seize on *one* view of us—usually a fairly simple, one-dimensional view—and maintain that view through all manner of evidence that the person has changed and grown.

We must constantly assert our own view of ourselves, based on an interior understanding of who we are and what we want out of our lives. If we don't, our systems define us, and our systems determine our goals. And our systems suck us into the Stress Cycle.

The tool for creating the Balance Cycle is a Personal Vision. Derived from a close objective and subjective structure for understanding yourself, a Personal Vision gives you solid ground to stand upon, a secure fulcrum to help you move your life, and a way to be sure it is *your* life you are living. As parents, we can give our children tools by our examples to help them understand themselves and separate their True Selves from System Selves, but *they* must step out in their lives and create their own Balance Cycles for themselves. No one can do it for them. Their lives will be different from ours. The Balance Cycle they create will of necessity be a different one than we created for ourselves. The underlying certainty, though, is that the more and sooner we create balance in *our* lives and understand ourselves, the more powerful are the tools our children will have to do the same in their lives. Any option we open for ourselves automatically becomes a possibility for our children.

PERSONAL VISION THROUGH THE CYCLE OF ADULT DEVELOPMENT

"Change is the only certainty." This wisdom comes to us from the past, but its lesson often eludes us. In any case, the cycle of adult development regularly alternates between change and stability.

Just as we must of necessity continually create and recreate the Balance Cycle for ourselves if we are to live in it, so must we periodically reassess our Personal Visions throughout our lives. A Personal Vision we create at age 17 before leaving for college can include certain areas of knowledge, like abilities, which don't change through our working lives. But a 17-year-old cannot create a Personal Vision that will work for a 25-year-old or a 30-year-old. The areas of experience that the 17-year-old cannot know are too many and too vast. Having a Personal Vision does not exempt us from the cycles of change; it just gives us a method for handling change more effectively.

We tend to make major changes in our lives and careers approximately every 20 years, starting in our early twenties. We tend to make minor changes and adjustments at the 10-year points. As noted by Sheehy and others, women may delay a mid-life change comparable to men's Mid-Life Transition for 10 years or so, effectively delaying the kind of change associated with mid-life until their fifties. However, we can usually look at our life spans as a series of 20-year cycles, with mid-point assessments and adjustments.

The jump from the security, structure and dependence of our families of origin to the way station of college and into independence in the work world is one of the largest we ever make. But the forces of change at mid-life are almost as great. Many people at mid-life literally set about recreating their careers from scratch, and many more wish they could. At the Mid-Life Transition, men and women have some advantages, in that they know so much more about themselves. They have such a wealth of experience to draw upon, and they are often socially and financially more stable. On the other hand, people at mid-life often feel trapped by these same factors. They know they shouldn't simply throw all of that out the window and start over. But they often wish to do so anyway.

At the Pre-Retirement Transition, we are once again faced with creating our lives over again. The lessons of the Mid-Life Transition continue to be important here. This Turning Point is just as inevitable as any other in our lives, and yet many people pretend it's just not going to happen. They think that if they have enough money saved up, that's all they need to consider.

The more gradual and continuous, rather than sudden and catastrophic, the change in your life, the better you will come out in the end. This is true even of great change such as the shift from work to retirement. If a young person's first job after college builds naturally out of college courses, internships and work experience in college, chances for success and satisfaction increase dramatically. At the Mid-Life Transition, if changes build naturally out of interests, plans, experiences and values of the thirties, then you are no longer dealing with a *crisis*, you are dealing with a natural time of transition and change. Plans for retirement can build out of relationships, interests and activities already in place long before actual retirement. Retirement can be an opportunity to express passions and values or play out major themes in one's life, but in a different way or in a different venue. *Continuity* in life helps lend it substance and meaning.

The Senior Transition is yet another inevitable focal point of re-creation. As the balance of your life shifts gradually from *doing* to *being*, the sense that you have focused on themes that are important to you enriches your moment-to-moment existence.

A PERSONAL VISION IN YOUR PRESENT CAREER

Most people who do the work of creating a Personal Vision and making it real find many good reasons for having chosen the career path they did. For most people, significant parts of their careers fit them well. As we have seen, when people start out in careers, their roles may initially fit well. As people progress in their careers, however, changes in themselves and rigidity in systems cause this fit to deteriorate. Feelings of stress, anger, boredom and lack of meaning follow. But regardless of the strength of these negative feelings about their present careers, a relatively small change in what they are doing or how they go about their careers can make a disproportionate difference in how they feel. A highly focused 10 percent shift in work roles—adding something new that you find meaningful or interesting or letting go of something you find tedious or difficult—can make a 100 percent difference in feelings. Moving from the Stress Cycle to the Balance Cycle does not mean turning your life upside down. Carefully assessing and integrating all of the important aspects of your life to arrive at a vision and making focused changes leads to balance. Unless you have done the work to create a Personal Vision, it is next to impossible to know exactly what to change to direct you toward balance. Not having a Personal Vision leaves you vulnerable to either persisting and enduring through life changes or making sudden and possibly ill-considered moves in response to overwhelming feelings of stress— both of which lead to notoriously unsatisfactory outcomes. Having a Personal Vision gives you a tool to use now and in the future to navigate change.

Let us look at those Turning Points at which we construct or reconstruct whole careers to see how Personal Vision impacts them.

A PERSONAL VISION TO CREATE A NEW CAREER

Young people must often choose a direction and begin their careers with very little information to go on. Considering that this is one of the most significant decisions anyone makes, it is surprising how little attention schools, colleges, corporations or the young people themselves pay to it.

Research has shown clearly that young people who have a positive vision for themselves in an attainable future are more likely to complete college on time and less likely to drop out or transfer. They make better grades, get more out of their college experiences, and feel happier, more satisfied and more enthusiastic about college. Later, they get better jobs that are more related to the work they did in college.

A Personal Vision begun in high school can frame and define a student's college experience. By figuring out what areas to explore in college—not an answer pulled out of a hat, but a real answer created and discovered *within*—students can know with a great deal more certainty what courses to take, what jobs and organizations to pursue on campus, which professors to contact, and what internships or summer jobs to attempt. Think of the experience of 18-year-olds who arrive on campus with no idea what they will do or what they want to accomplish in school (the majority). Taking one course after another with no idea how this work could relate to their lives, forced to declare majors for more or less random reasons, or feeling compelled to decide upon a career such as medicine with virtually no knowledge of what that involves, it's no surprise that the majority do not finish in four years. The wonder is that any finish at all.

These students are all victims of the Lemming Conspiracy. Unless they work purposefully to create a Personal Vision, they will continue to be victims throughout their lives and eventually add their lives to the statistics concerning stress, burnout and boredom.

The rare student who has a plan—one carefully constructed from self-discovery and from first-hand experience of life—stands out from this common herd. More focused, more sure, more confident, able to benefit fully from what college offers, these students appear to cut through life more easily than most. Perhaps by accident or family encouragement, they have created something like a Personal Vision; they have just done the work. But *this does not have to be an accident*. Anyone can create a Personal Vision. And a Personal Vision can transform anyone's life.

To some extent, we create new careers every 20 years. The 41-year-old at mid-life is in just as much a quandary about what to do as the 20-year-old college student, or the 62-year-old facing retirement. At these major bends in our life streams, we need some connection to the territory ahead. We need a vision that connects ourselves as we are now to a future that makes sense. This is the job of a Personal Vision. There is no short cut. The process for creating a Personal Vision merely helps it emerge and helps make it useful to you.

One of the most interesting aspects of Personal Vision is its use to corporations. The next section describes how corporations can use the idea of the whole person to create more human—and more profitable—organizations.

PERSONAL VISION IN THE WORKPLACE

Stress pervades most people's working days. The higher you go, the more stress takes its toll. The workplace does not encourage families to thrive, nourish values or produce people who live full lives.

Employees grow and change. They arrive at Turning Points and want more meaning. It is no accident that executive derailments, transfers, and loss almost invariably happen at Turning Points. Corporations cannot provide Personal Visions for employees, but they can provide conditions in which employees can create their own.

As we have seen, businesses have difficulty seeing the interests of their employees as being in some ways the same as the bottom-line interests of the business itself. In all cases, the responsibility for living a fulfilling and satisfying life rests with the employee, not the corporation. Recently, however, some researchers have documented that there is a strong and replicable connection between satisfied customers and satisfied employees. Businesses have found that, by retaining more key employees, they also retain more of the vital relationships between the business and its customers. Even small increases in customer retention translates to very large percentage gains in profitability and business health.

Investors pay attention to these connections. It has become apparent that satisfied employees mean increased efficiency and profitability, and this fact has assumed greater importance in investment decisions.

So what makes an employee fulfilled and satisfied? Money? Prestige? Power? *None* of these aspects of work makes it even into the top seven factors that influence employee satisfaction and retention. The key to retaining key employees? Balance and meaning.

People want to have whole lives. They want families and communities, and they want to feel productive and useful out in the world. When they don't have this balance, and don't see any prospect for attaining it, they hit Turning Points and leave. Or they hit Turning Points and become less involved in work, or less satisfied with it.

Companies can't dictate whole lives. There is no set of commandments they can lay down, no matter how liberal or enlightened, to insure that employees achieve balance. It is only individual people who can examine their own lives and decide what they want to do.

Companies can help. In the rare cases in which companies actively encourage employees to do the work of creating Personal Visions, effectiveness, efficiency and profitability increase.

This also creates the new corporation. The new corporation does not work through the traditional totalitarian hierarchy.

In the traditional hierarchy, responsibility resides at the top. Orders and direction pass down the pyramid to the bottom. In this paternal model, if you keep your nose clean and do as you're told, you don't have anything to worry about. Daddy will do the thinking, and Daddy will take care of you.

The old model of corporation produced massive inefficiency, abuse and excess. In this model, the executive at the top—the one making all the decisions and taking all the responsibility—could and should make tens of millions of dollars while at the same time closing plants and laying off workers because of lack of profitability.

The new corporation is more efficient. It engages in a dialogue with the employee. The corporation says, in effect, "This is what I need you to do, and this is what I'm willing to pay for that service." The employee says, "This is who I am, and this is what I can do well and in a way satisfying to me, and this is what I am willing to do." The new element is *choice*, an element so powerful and effective that it transforms the corporation. What choice creates is the difference between someone who comes to work and just does a job and someone who *likes* to go to work because it creates *meaning* in life. "My work expresses who I am."

THE LEMMING CONSPIRACY AND LEADING A TRUE LIFE

The positive power of systems makes civilizations possible. All of the advances in culture, comfort, productivity, security, longevity and health that civilization delivers were made available to us all through systems. However, individuals do not *live* in systems. They exist. They play a role. They provide a function. The real life of a person happens individually on the inside.

Creativity, energy, passion, wit and life are only expressed by individuals. The more we can express that part of ourselves, the more fully human we become. We do not see the choice as either/or: "Either you express your true self, or you exist as an automaton of the system." Like most black-and-white statements, this is not a true choice.

It is possible to express a True Self *and* to fulfill your function as a member of systems. The difficult part is attending to the whole person. That is what we created the process in this book to do. Once you have delineated that True Self and figured out a Personal Vision to express it, it becomes entirely possible to find a place for that Personal Vision in systems. People almost always have many more choices in life *after* they create a Personal Vision than before. Why? Is it because Personal Visions create more options? No, all the options were always there. Rather, Personal Visions help them focus on what they really want. When you know what you are after, you can almost always find it.

The Lemming Conspiracy keeps you from seeing yourself, and it keeps you from seeing the true options for your life. By keeping you focused on a System Self, believing that *this* is all there is, the Lemming Conspiracy limits you. A Personal Vision is a way to find and express your True Self. Once you can communicate it to others you have the option—the real choice—of expressing your True Self every day in the life you lead.

"I have learned this, at least, by my experiments; that if one advances confidently in the direction of his dreams, and endeavors to live the life he has imagined, he will meet with a success unexpected in common hours."

Henry David Thoreau, WALDEN

This book was not written to be a technical reference. However, readers who wish to pursue some of the subjects of this book are referred to the following excellent resources.

Amabile, T. M. *The Social Psychology of Creativity*. New York: Springer-Verlag, 1983. Excellent summary of research on creativity.

Bertalanffy, Ludwig Von. *General System Theory: Foundations, Development, Application*. New York: George Braziller, 1976. Highly theoretical treatment of the general properties and workings of any system.

Bowen, Murray. *Family Therapy in General Practice*. New York: Aronson, 1978. Readers are referred specifically to Chapters 20, 21, and 22 for an excellent general treatment of differentiation from the family of origin.

Caine, R. N., and Caine, G. *Making Connections: Teaching and the Human Brain*. Alexandria, Va.: Association for Supervision and Curriculum Development, 1991. Practical treatment of goals and behavior, showing how internally motivated goals provide much more power for learning and behavior.

Campbell, Joseph. *The Hero with a Thousand Faces*. Princeton: Bollingen, 1949. Description of the process of change.

Covey, Stephen R. *The Seven Habits of Highly Effective People*. New York: Simon and Schuster, 1990. The classic work on values and their impact at work.

Csikszentmihalyi, Mihaly. *Flow: The Psychology of Optimal Experience*. New York: HarperCollins, 1990. A readable treatment of what it means to live a life expressive of one's True Self.

Erikson, Erik. *Childhood and Society*. New York: Norton, 1964 (reissued, 1993). One of the first works to propose stages of development beyond childhood.

Eysenck, H. J., and Eysenck, M. W. *Personality and*

Individual Differences: A Natural Science Approach.
New York: Plenum, 1985. A classic work on personality
research and theory.

Gall, John. *Systemantics: How Systems Work and How They
Fail*. Ann Arbor, Mich.: General Systemantics Press, 1986. A
highly readable description of the workings of human
systems.

Gardner, Howard. *Frames of Mind: The Theory of Multiple
Intelligences*. New York: Basic Books, 1983. Theoretical
treatment of abilities, as opposed to traditional ideas about
general intelligence.

Gawain, S. *Creative Visualization*. Berkeley, Calif.: New
World Library, 1978. An excellent explanation of creativity.

Gazzaniga, M. S. *The Social Brain*. New York: Basic Books,
1985. A scientific examination of goal-setting and behavior.

Koestler, Arthur. *The Act of Creation*. New York: Macmillan,
1964. An excellent treatment of the *process* of creativity.

Levinson, Daniel J. *The Seasons of a Man's Life*. New York:
Alfred A. Knopf, 1978.

——, with Judy D. Levinson. *The Seasons Of A Woman's Life*.
New York: Alfred A. Knopf, 1996. Pioneering research
on adult life span. Ground-breaking observations on the
regularity of adult developmental stages.

Lowman, Rodney L. *The Clinical Practice of Career
Assessment*. Washington, D.C.: American Psychological
Association, 1991. Describes the state of research with
regard to abilities, interests and personality.

McCrae, R. M., and Costa, P. T. *Personality in Adulthood*.
New York: Guilford Press, 1990. Offers a five-factor theory
of personality, considered the most complete treatment.

Sheehy, Gail. *Passages*. New York: Dutton, 1976.

——. *New Passages*. New York: Random House, 1995.
Highly accessible works describing adult development
through the life span.

Sternberg, R. J. *The Triarchic Mind: A New Theory of
Human Intelligence*. New York: Viking, 1988. Another

presentation of the idea of human abilities as opposed to general intelligence.

READINGS ON PERSONAL VISION

Campbell, Angus. *The Sense of Well-Being in America*. New York: McGraw-Hill, 1981.

Cousins, N. *Head First: The Biology of Hope*. New York: Dutton, 1989.

McClelland, David C. "Achievement Motivation Can Be Developed." *Harvard Business Review*, November, 1965.

Myers, David. *The Pursuit of Happiness*. New York: Avon, 1992.

Petri, H. L. *Motivation*. Belmont, Calif.: Wadsworth, 1991.

Seligman, Martin E. P. *Learned Optimism*. New York: Knopf, 1991.

Strack, Fritz, Michael Argyle, and Norbert Schwarz, eds. *Subjective Well-Being: An Interdisciplinary Perspective*. Oxford, England: Pergamon Press, 1990.

Super, Donald. *The Psychology of Careers*. New York: Harper, 1957.

———. *Career Development: Self-Concept Theory*. Princeton, N.J.: College Board, 1963.

———, ed. *Life Roles, Values, and Careers*. New York: Jossey Bass, 1995.

SPECIAL OFFER FOR PURCHASERS
OF THIS BOOK

As you can read in Chapter 4, your natural talents and abilities — your inborn gifts that make some tasks as natural as play and others seem like frustrating labor — are an important and foundational element to finding your best career fit. The Thought Experiment in that chapter shows you how to guess at your most important natural abilities. However, to really pay off the idea of finding your True Self and expressing it in your work and career, we would like to make this special offer for purchasers of this book. We would like you to be able to experience the entire Highlands Ability Battery, receive a two-hour individual feedback conference from one of our specially-trained counselors, and have a comprehensive written report for $75 off of the regular price of the Battery.

The Highlands Ability Battery is an objective series of twenty-three work samples that can tell you much about the kinds of roles and tasks for which you are most naturally suited. The value of having objective information about your natural abilities, as opposed to self-report data, is considerable.

As you may read in this book, abilities can't tell you what to do or not to do. They are one of many important factors to include when figuring out what you want to do with your life, but they are the best place to start.

$75 Off Regular Price
of
The Highlands Ability Battery

To take advantage of this offer, bring this book to the nearest Highlands Program office. To find the Highlands Program office nearest to you, you may either call the 800 number below, or go to our home page on the World Wide Web.

Telephone: 1-800-373-0083
World Wide Web: www.highlandsprogram.com